Drunk on the Wine
of the Beloved

غزل

بار دگر گفته‌ام و باز دگر می‌گویم

هر من حال شدم این ره نه بخود می‌پویم

دیر بر آینه طوطی صفتم داشته‌اند

آنچه استاد ازل گفت بگو می‌گویم

من اگر خارم و گر گل چمن آرایی هست

هر آنک دلبرم می‌پرورد من می‌رویم

دوستان عیب من بی‌دل شیدا مکنید

گوهری دارم و صاحب نظری می‌جویم

گرچه با دلق ملمع می‌گلگون عیب است

مکنم عیب کزاد رنگ ریا می‌شویم

خنده و گریه عشاق ز جائی دگرست

می‌سرایم بشب و وقت سحر می‌مویم

حافظم گفت دهن خاک درینجا نه سبو

گو مکن عیب که من مشک ختن می‌بویم

Drunk on the Wine of the Beloved

100 Poems of Hafiz

Translations by Thomas Rain Crowe

SHAMBHALA
Boulder
2001

Shambhala Publications, Inc.
2129 13th Street
Boulder, Colorado 80302
www.shambhala.com
©2001 by Thomas Rain Crowe

Some of the poems in this collection first appeared in the following publications: *Nexus* vols. 20 (Fall 1994), 32 (Fall 1997): *Oxygen; International Poetry Review;* and *WP Journal* (Ireland). The following poems appeared originally in *In Wineseller's Street*, published by Ibex Publishers (Bethesda, Md., 1998, ISBN 0-936347-67-8), and are reprinted by permission: O Pilgrim, O Preacher, The Monks in the Monastery, No Guarantees, Nothing, and The Essence of Grace.

The frontispiece (page ii) is ghazal 22 in Farsi. From Mehdi Nakosteen, *The Ghazaliyyat of Haafez of Shiraz* (Boulder: Este Es press, 1973), page 68. Thomas Crowe's translation appears under the title "I've Said It Before and I'll Say It Again."

Printed in the United States of America

Shambhala Publications makes every effort to print on acid-free, recycled paper.

Shambhala Publications is distributed worldwide by Penguin Random House, Inc., and its subsidiaries.

LIBRARY OF CONGRESS CATALOGING-IN-PUBLICATION DATA

Hafiz, 14th cent.
   [Divan. English. Selections]
   Drunk on the wine of the beloved : 100 poems of Hafiz /
   translations by Thomas Rain Crowe.—1st ed.
      p. cm.
   Includes bibliographical references.
   ISBN 978-1-57062-853-5 (pbk.)
      I. Crowe, Thomas Rain. II. Title.

PK6465.Z31 C7613 2001
891'.5511—dc21   2001020886

To my mother and father: the beloved

Contents

Acknowledgments

MY PRIMARY translation source was *The Divan-i-Hafiz*, translated by H. Wilberforce Clarke (1891; reprint London, 1974). Other sources are:

Arberry, A. J. *Fifty Poems of Hafiz* (1947). Cambridge, 1962.
Hafiz: Selections from the Rubaiyat and Odes. Translated by a
    member of the Persia Society of London. London, 1920.
McCarthy, Justin Huntly. *Ghazels from the Divan of Hafiz*.
    London, 1893.
Nakosteen, Mehdi. *The Ghazaliyyat of Haafez of Shiraz*.
    Boulder, 1973.
Smith, Paul. *Divan of Hafiz*. Melbourne, 1983.

Special thanks to Meher Spiritual Center for the place and quiet time in which to find, again, the (illusive) voice of Hafiz; Kendra Crossen Burroughs as the guardian angel and editor of this book; Dennis McCabe for his open invitation and a stage for Hafiz's voice; Michael Beeby for the gift of the Wilberforce Clarke *Divan*; Nan Watkins, Sal D'Angio, Chris Rosser, and Safed Fareed for giving the poems a musical dimension in performance; Himayat Inayati, Abi'l Khayr, and the Sufi Healing Order for the push; Farhad Shirzad for a first home; Bhau Kalchuri for the nothing and the everything; Bobi Jones for the enthusiasm and passion; Jem and Demir Williford, Shaykh Sherif Baba, and the Rifa'i-Marufi Sufi Order of America for the support, the zikrs, and the "Bedouin cannonball"; and the grapes, for all that wine!

Introduction

F OR THE MAJORITY OF THOSE LIVING in Iran, Iraq, Turkey, India, and much of the Islamic world, Shamsuddin Muhammad-i-Hafiz-i-Shiraz, known simply as Hafiz, is considered to be the greatest poet of all time. Since his death around 1389, his legendary status has continued down through the centuries, inspiring praise from Western literary luminaries such as Goethe ("In his poetry Hafiz has inscribed undeniable truth indelibly — Hafiz has no peer!"), Emerson ("Hafiz fears nothing. He sees too far to see; such is the only man I wish to see or be . . ."), and Lorca ("Hafiz's ghazals are sublime!"). And some spiritual authorities have declared that Hafiz was not only a great poet but a spiritually advanced mystic as well. The modern Indian spiritual leader Meher Baba identified Hafiz as a fully realized Perfect Master and said, "There is no equal to Hafiz in poetry. His *Divan* is the best book in the world because it engenders feelings which ultimately lead to illumination."

Hafiz is said to have been a Sufi, but in truth his "religion" was the love of God and the expression of that love. No spiritual institution could contain him, although his popularity has grown so since his death that even orthodox Muslims have claimed him as one of their own. In fact, Hafiz often criticized the false Sufis who wore rags to draw attention to themselves, as well as those who wore fine blue robes and paraded their holiness in the marketplace. Perhaps no other poet from any time or tradition has equaled Hafiz in his outspokenness against deceit and hypocrisy at all levels of society. The ghazals of his *Divan*, or collection of poems, are rife with such criticism, often scathingly sarcastic if not downright confrontational.

But there is another side to the poems of Hafiz—a softer, more spiritually sensitive side that is the principal reason why he was loved by so many during his lifetime and by millions in the centuries that followed. Hazrat Inayat Khan, the founder of the Sufi Movement of the West, wrote: "The work of Hafiz, from beginning to end, is one series of beautiful pictures, ever revealing and most inspiring. Once a person has studied Hafiz he has reached the top of the mountain, from whence he beholds the sublimity of the immanence of God." And Paul Smith ventures in the introduction to his *Book of the Winebringer* that "if God had taken form as a Poet, it seems He would have been happy to have written as Hafiz wrote."

Despite Hafiz's high profile in the East, his work is little known in the West. In the last one hundred years or more, only a few scholars, military adventurers, and poet-anthologists have tried their hand at bringing, as best they could, the poetry of Hafiz to an English-speaking audience. But in no case that I have seen have any of the translations or versions been true to both the literary form of the ghazal and the distinctive voice of what I would call "the original." While this may be seen as a credit to the complexity and subtleties of Hafiz's work—as well as an example of the difficulty of importing a literary form of the East articulately to the West—it is still somewhat curious that, especially in the last fifty years, there haven't been more attempts to give this great poet's work a more accessible modern narrative voice, one that would speak to the masses of today much as it did to those during his own time.

After Hafiz's death, two collections of his ghazals and other poems were assembled. One of these, compiled by a young student of his named Sayyid Kasim-i-Anvar (died 1431), consisted of 569 ghazals and was called the *Divan-i-Khwaja-i-Hafiz*, a work that is considered by poets and scholars alike to be the peak of perfection of the ghazal form.

Ghazals were originally lyrical poems recited or sung by minstrels in the royal courts of pre-Islamic Iran. The word *ghazal* is of Arabic origin and means "love song," and even today many of Hafiz's ghazals, set to music, are performed as popular songs in Iran, Turkey, and India. A unique verse form, the ghazal is usually between five and fifteen *beyts*, or lines of verse split into two equal parts—what we in the West think of as couplets. The rhyme appears at the end of each line and repeats throughout the entire poem. As an innovator, Hafiz did much to change the existing ghazal form of his day to suit his needs. He is known, for instance, for inventing an internal rhyme structure, producing an effect that is chantlike in its repetition of words and sounds.

Hafiz also revolutionized the ghazal by making the focus and subject matter more populist, political, and personal, and by adding greater emphasis to the final couplet containing the poet's name. The Persian practice of including the poet's pseudonym, or *takhallus*, in the last couplet can be traced back as far as the first half of the sixth century and was used as a device by which the poet could be identified with his work. All of Hafiz's innovations to this poetic form made his work (and the work that followed) more accessible to audiences, opening up more windows and doors to the voice and presence of God.

Almost all of Hafiz's ghazals contain sentiments of romantic love, images of nature, and moral counsel. But the overriding subject is love of God, symbolized by the metaphor of wine. In Hafiz's case, the ghazals are used mainly as a vehicle or voice to express his divine longing. This love and longing is represented in his work symbolically in many ways and in many guises, in keeping with the rigors of the ghazal "rules" of the time. The metaphor of wine, for instance, while referring principally to divine love, can also mean truth, grace, or knowledge, while the metaphor of the wineglass or cup is a direct reference to the heart. So, when Hafiz says, "O Winebringer, fill my cup to the brim with your best wine," he is really saying: "O God, pour your divine love into my heart!" In this collection, such endearing occupational surnames as Winebringer, Winemaker, and Wineseller are all allusions to God, or, more particularly, His representative in the human form of the master. "The Beloved" is an even more direct reference to the spiritual master who is one with God. And here it might be useful to note that in Farsi the pronouns do not indicate gender, making the business of translating all this longing and love somewhat nonspecific in relation to gender or sex, literalness or symbology. While this ambiguousness only adds to the mysteriousness and cosmic consciousness of Hafiz's voice, I have followed in the footsteps of other translators in leaving it up to the mind and persuasion of readers to make these gender associations for themselves, as it suits their own preferences.

In a similar vein, there may be questions as to who or what, in fact, "the Beloved" is in Hafiz's mind. Symbolically, the Beloved appears at times in the guise of the rose, the sun, the falcon, the Friend, the Painter, the Architect, and the Gardener, in whose Garden the lover and the Beloved meet. (Although there is no capitalization of words in Farsi as in English, I have capitalized pronouns such as *You* and *He* to indicate that Hafiz is addressing the Beloved or God.) In these conversations or meetings, the lover may appear as the moth, the slave, the pearl diver, or the nightingale. The field (the physical world) upon which the game of love is played can be the desert (waiting, longing, thirst), the sea (the ocean of love or turbulence), or the sky (change, fate). Regardless of the venue, the waxing and waning love affair between lover (Hafiz) and the Beloved (God) continues. . . .

Other important and often-repeated symbols appear throughout these poems: the Breeze (the messenger of God, usually bearing good news or divine inspiration), the Boat (the vehicle that carries the lover to union with God), the Winehouse (the place a lover of God goes to be with the Beloved), the Moon (physical beauty), the Nightingale (the poet, bard), the Parrot (the unenlightened, and/or the followers of religion). While some of these images may not be particularly "modern" in a twenty-first-century American sense, they are universally accessible enough to have allowed me to leave them intact in the midst of my more contemporary language. If I had manipulated these symbolic images too drastically (or at all), I felt, I'd be running the risk of misrepresenting or missing altogether the deeper original meanings of these symbols that Hafiz uses to repeatedly emphasize the profound nature of his criticisms as well as his longing and his love.

While much of the action of these ghazals takes place in the Winehouse or in Wineseller's Street, and much of the talk is of wine and drunkenness, with cup or glass in hand, we must be careful not to read too much literalness into these scenes, even though it may be familiar and fun to do so. The Winehouse of Hafiz's ghazals is clearly not simply a tavern or bar, and the winedrinkers to whom Hafiz directs his monologues are rarely common drunks. Hafiz's recitations of his poems usually took place, as far as we know, in the context of spiritual or literary gatherings where music and poetry were a customary pastime.

Because wine was and is forbidden to pious Muslims, this particular poetic image becomes even more potent in the context of Hafiz's Winehouse poems. All this superimposed "decadence" was used merely as a kind of camouflage for the deeper spiritual messages hidden beneath the veil of symbolic imagery. The ultimate effect was that the poems reached a larger and more diverse audience, especially, in centuries following the fourteenth, the peasant and working classes.

Just as Hafiz revolutionized the ghazal form, making it more accessible to his audiences, so, too, have I attempted to bring them comfortably to the modern reader, through familiar American speech and narrative rhythms. In doing so, I have leaped, fully conscious, into a controversy of my own—the business of "versioning" or, more to the point, translating from a nonoriginal language source. Since the mid-1960s, when it became first popular in the United States for poets who were not fluent linguists to do "versions" or "renderings" of poems from other cultures already poorly or academically and unpoetically translated into English, the debate has raged between the two camps over the legitimacy of such a process. While the academics embrace literalness and the artists prefer a more poetic and/or populist text, the standard dictionaries of the day use the terms "translation," "rendering," and "version" interchangeably and consistently—making the whole argument a semantic one and in the end a waste of everyone's time when the real issue is to find ways to bring poetic and spiritual credibility and relevance from one era and readership to another.

In my case, I have done my transformative work (which one would hope might be transfigurative as well), trying to remain true to the original couplet form while, at the same time, breaking down the strict meter and rhyme rules in favor of a free and open verse form. This lends itself to the profound power of Hafiz's narrative poetic message, thus bringing the work to a novice English-speaking readership. And since Hafiz was considered to be, first and foremost, an oral poet, these versions were translated in such a way as to be read aloud—much like the poems of Dylan Thomas or Vachel Lindsay.

In defense of my versioning efforts, I should cite the inherent problems of translating anything from fourteenth-century Persian into a modern American idiom. Time, culture, and outdated forms are the hurdles that any translator of this conversion must face. Aside from the fact that no poem can successfully be translated literally and to perfection from one tongue to another, the least we can do is to give our poets some sort of literal text to work with in their efforts to carry the translated poet's spirit and voice into a more modern age and a foreign environment.

In bringing these poems from the *Divan* trans-nationally (and trans-rationally) into an American idiom, not the least of my problems was giving a lyric personality a narrative face. Confronting this and the other hurdles I have alluded to, my process consisted in taking the scholarship of Wilberforce Clarke and trying to create a believable, if not authentic, blend of fourteenth-century Islamic spirituality and twenty-first century American sensibility—in essence, trying to create a bridge to our own century and to bring an engaging yet valid impersonator of Hafiz over that time bridge. In some cases, I have sought to retain the rhythmic flavor of the ghazal form by incorporating, from time to time, spontaneous and intuitive rhymes that seem to be loyal to the meaning of the original text as presented by Clarke. In this sense, and not unlike Hafiz himself during his own time, I have created an amalgam of the old and the new and a unique American ghazal form consisting of rhythmic open-verse couplets that adhere to many, if not most, of the contemporary and familiar American forms, as well as the idiosyncrasies of the ghazal. And it is here, through this new lyric-narrative hybrid, that Hafiz speaks . . . and in speaking, brings his dervish, dancelike poems to life!

Wine and Love

Meher Baba

THE SUFI MASTER POETS often compared love with wine. Wine is the most fitting figure for love because both intoxicate. But while wine causes self-forgetfulness, love leads to Self-realization.

The behavior of the drunkard and the lover are similar; each disregards the world's standards of conduct and each is indifferent to the opinion of the world. But there are worlds of difference between the course and the goal of the two: the one leads to subterranean darkness and denial; the other gives wings to the soul for its flight to freedom.

The drunkenness of the drunkard begins with a glass of wine which elates his spirit and loosens his affections and gives him a new view of life that promises a forgetfulness from his daily worries. He goes on from a glass to two glasses, to a bottle; from companionship to isolation, from forgetfulness to oblivion—oblivion which in Reality is the Original state of God, but which, with the drunkard, is an empty stupor—and he sleeps in a bed or in a gutter. And he awakens in a dawn of futility, an object of disgust and ridicule to the world.

The lover's drunkenness begins with a drop of God's love which makes him forget the world. The more he drinks, the closer he draws to his Beloved, and the more unworthy he feels of the Beloved's love; and he longs to sacrifice his very life at the Beloved's feet. He, too, does not know whether he sleeps on a bed or in a gutter, and becomes an object of ridicule to the world; but he rests in bliss, and God the Beloved takes care of his body, and neither the elements nor disease can touch it.

One out of many such lovers sees God face to face. His longing becomes infinite; he is like a fish thrown up on the beach, leaping and squirming to regain the ocean. He sees God everywhere and in everything, but he cannot find the gate of union. The Wine that he drinks turns into Fire in which he continuously burns in blissful agony. And the Fire eventually becomes the Ocean of Infinite Consciousness in which he drowns.

Drunk on the Wine
of the Beloved

O Pilgrim

O pilgrim, come and look into the mirror of this glass of wine!

And pick up your net, the Pure Bird can never be caught.
There is nothing in this cage but wind.

Live for the moment! When the water in the lake dried up,
Even Adam left the Garden of Safe Joy.

At the Mardi Gras of Life, have one or two cups of wine, then leave.
Don't hang around waiting for an enlightened drunk!

Say to your heart: "My youth is gone."
Even though you have picked no roses, use your old head skillfully,
    then do the right thing.

The puritan know-it-all never sees the drunkard
Or secrets hidden behind the veil.

O Wise One, those of us who sit all day on Your threshold have more than
Earned our pay. For service rendered, to pay Your slaves in pity is OK.

When I handed the reins of my heart to You,
I gave up, forever, any hope of becoming anything other than a horse.

O student of the cup of Hafiz: drink! And then go like the wind
To the Master, and tell him the story of this great wine!

Look at This Beauty

The beauty of this poem is beyond words.
Do you need a guide to experience the heat of the sun?

Blessed is the brush of the painter who paints
Such beautiful pictures for his virgin bride.

Look at this beauty. There is no reason for what you see.
Experience its grace. Even in nature there is nothing so fine.

Either this poem is a miracle, or some sort of magic trick,
Guided either by Gabriel or the Invisible Voice, inside.

No one, not even Hafiz, can describe with words the Great Mystery.
No one knows in which shell the priceless pearl does hide.

Writing in Code

O morning breeze, bring your happy face as soon as you can
To the Beloved's Street!

You are the Messenger of Mystery, and now I know I am on the
Right path. So don't give me orders, but urge me gently on.

Winebringer, give me some of your reddest wine,
As my soul is slipping from my hands.

Let me tie all my hope to Your woven gold belt.
This diet of reason I've been on has led me nowhere.
That waistline of Yours traces a divine subtlety. Now I know.

From where I sit, the sight of Your sword is a sure sign of drought,
So take me captive and slay me with water and buckets of ice.

I have written these words in code, made only for Your eyes.
Please take them, and read them right away!

For Hafiz, speaking Turkish and Arabic are like talking in the same tongue:
He tells Love's story in every language that he knows!

A Bucket of Wine

O Winebringer, bring us a bucket of wine,
For it's morning and the dew is falling from the sky.

Friends, drink all the blood from this bucket;
It's not against the law and it's something we all can do.

If you wake up tomorrow with headache or hangover,
Drink more wine, and chase this discomfort away.

Winebringer, don't go far from this Winehouse,
For grief is waiting for you out behind that rock.

Minstrel, play us some more of your happy songs
To keep those greedy demons at bay.

More wine! The music of the harp is whispering in my ear:
It sings, "Be happy; and always listen to what this old Master has to say."

Hafiz, stop your crying. The plant that is your longing drank
Blood, and made fruit. Why do you want to pull this plant, now,
    from the ground?

Half-Hearted Hugs

O minstrel, please compose a sweet melody in Persian
That I can sing!

The sound of the harp and the Winebringer's clapping
Have brought back sweet memories of my youth.

And give some wine to my friends
So that they can be happy, too!

Winebringer, come here, and bring me a quart of wine!
God would not want me drinking from this little cup.

Let's all join in together in singing these songs,
So that Your jubilation can be shared.

The spring of my life has been spent, and has passed, in His care;
In this time of togetherness, may He watch over us all!

O Beloved, because of my blindness, I have missed many chances
To be with You: and now I am older, and alone.

The Winemaker's daughter would make a beautiful bride, but
Her beauty is a sure sign of yet more separation and divorce.

Even Christ, who was always Himself, had the sense to
Take the Sun to be His bride.

At my age, youth no longer has any appeal;
I only get kindly kisses and half-hearted hugs from these beautiful girls.

Do not think that I am angry just because I cry. Remember:
The seas and oceans all come from the source of a very small stream.

It is not always our fate to be surrounded by happy and adoring friends;
To Hafiz, the poems of Persia sound like sad, sad songs.

I Heard the Rumor

Thank God that you have shown me Your face! Like the sun,
Your beauty has blinded my sense of destiny and given me sight.

In the gallery of my heart, I have painted portraits of loneliness
In colors that predict the day when You will come.

When the sun is hot on my head because of Your love,
The Pure Bird of Destiny throws His shadow on me to keep me cool.

I heard the rumor You were coming, so I have been busy saying prayers.
I needed this respite of joy for my aching heart.

O Beloved, knock hard on the handle when you finally come to my door;
I have left the light on in the window, and this house is meant for You!

The Gambler

The condition of the winedrinker is happiness; he doesn't know
Whether it is he, his head, or his hat that he has thrown away.

The fundamentalist fanatic is ignorant because of all that he desires;
It is only when he takes up the winecup that enlightenment prevails.

During the day, be a skillful artist;
For at night the darkness will reflect a heart that's weak.

Only in morning can a glass of splendid wine taste good
And throw its protective rays around the horizon of your house.

But be careful who you drink with:
The censor and the critic will repay your generosity by replacing the wine
    in your glass with sticks and stones.

O Hafiz, the sun is coming up in the corner of the Winehouse.
Lift up your head. With the full moon on your shoulder,
    the time to gamble with loaded dice   is now!

O Preacher

O preacher, what is all this commotion? Go about your own work.
My heart fell from my hands long ago. What is wrong with your job?

The link between man and the Beloved, which God created from nothing,
Is something that no high priest or scholar can explain.

The beggar in Winestreet is free of the eight houses of Paradise.
He that is bound and captive by You is free from both worlds.

Even though I am drunk with love, and ruined,
I have grown healthy from drinking that wine.

O my heart, stop your complaining, you are not a battered spouse!
Your Lover has warned you again and again of this pain.

Like wind in my ear, or like lips that caress the reed of a flute,
If You are caressing my wish, I will not turn my back on the world.

Hafiz, go, explain no more stories and recite no more magical verse.
If they haven't gotten the message yet, don't waste your breath.
Turn your lips, instead, to the face of the Beloved!

Worthless

A rose that isn't the Beloved's face is worthless;
A spring that is not made of wine is worthless too.

The fences around the fields and the breeze blowing in gardens
Without the Beloved's tulip cheek are worth nothing and without grace.

What use are sugary lips and roses that look like God,
Without His kiss or smothering embrace?

The dance of the swaying cypress and the rapture of the rose,
Without the nightingale's songs, are worthless.

O Gardener, every picture that the hands of intellect have drawn
Is useless unless they have traced Your face.

So, if you are drinking wine or sitting in the garden with roses
Instead of seeking the Beloved, then you are wasting time.

Hafiz, your life is nothing more than a tarnished old coin,
Traded again and again for others to deface. Don't you have
    something better you can do?

I've Got Everything I Need

Not even Shangrila is more beautiful
Than being in Winehouse Street.

So why should I keep hiding all my desires?
With this jug of wine and this beautiful place, I've got everything I need.

I belong here in His house and in the fields of my native land
Where I get pleasure from looking at lovely faces and enchanting eyes.

Are you listening? Is there no one else this mad?
My words, though they may sound sweet, are really useless and vain.

Be respectful when you talk of the Master's abode,
For not even a brahmin or a dervish knows of these things.

O Beloved, there is no room left in my heart
For anything but You!

Please show pity on poor Hafiz. He is wounded and in pain.
Even if he seems happy today, he is waiting for sunlight, and all it ever
seems to do   is rain.

I Said

To the Beloved I said: "You have made a thoughtless mistake."
He said: "What more could I do? It was fate."

I said: "Others have cited many faults against You."
He said: "Accusations on the page of the forehead is all they were."

I said: "To this day, the evil ones associate with Your name."
He said: "This has been the burden of my ill-fortune and bad luck."

I said: "O Moon, why have you cut off from me your love?"
He said: "From where I sit, the sky was full of wrath and ill-will."

I said: "Up till now, you drank this wine with joy!"
He said: "In the last cup I drank, was the cure."

I said: "Where, then, did your life go so quickly?"
He said: "What else could I do? Life is not infinite, but definite."

I said: "But God gave you the desire to unite with Him!"
He said: "Union with God was not my desire, is not my only purpose."

I said: "You sure took your time to get there!"
He said: "Perhaps in my lingering was time's good counsel."

I said: "Why, then, have you gone so far away from Hafiz?"
He said: "The road I live on always goes this way."

Listen to My Pen's Advice

O Beloved, why do you treat us this way?
For too long we have been ignored and deprived of Your light.

Pilgrim, listen to my pen's advice, for this pearl of wisdom is worth
More than all your suffering or your gold.

O Winebringer, bring wine to those drinkers who are mad for more wine,
That is, if You have any of last night's good wine left.

But I want to know how are You going to show us Your face,
With the light of the sun and moon reflecting in our eyes?

O philosopher, be sensible and don't speak out against love,
Have you some sort of bone to pick with God?

Aren't you at all afraid of my burning sigh,
Standing there in that cotton coat so close to the flames?

Hafiz, yours is the most beautiful verse I have ever heard,
You must have the Koran and the Bible in your heart, combined!

There Is Nothing in This Well but Wind

I'm drunk again on the wine of love—Winebringer, bring more wine!
And fill up my cup, for without wine this party will be no fun.

My love won't even penetrate that veil covering the Beloved's face;
So Minstrel, give us a melody, and Winebringer, bring us some more wine!

To get in this place, I bent my body into the shape of a doorknocker, so
That the doorman wouldn't send me away to another door.

Together, all of us here are hoping to see His face;
Together, all of us are waiting with our vain hopes, our vain fancies, and
   our vain dreams.

Drunk from Your gaze, I lust for Your ruby lips.
I have been reduced to less than a question, which in the end is less than
   my vain dreams.

Because no one can look directly at the sun,
I have asked the eye of my heart: what is the use of all this worrying?

So don't waste your time trying to fill your cup with water
When you know that there is nothing in this well but wind.

O Hafiz, in this desert, you have fallen victim to your own illusions.
When was a pilgrim's thirst ever quenched by a mirage?

Let Me Tell You the Truth

When Your shadow fell on my head,
Fortune and prosperity became my slaves.

Since then, years have passed, and that old fortune has passed away;
And now I'm asleep in Your bed.

Don't think that because my eyes are open, I'm awake;
I'm only waiting and watching to see Your face in my dreams.

Let me tell you the truth: I have spent my life grieving for You;
Even so, I have never spent one moment alone.

Ask any physician and he'll tell you there is no cure for my pain.
Without the Beloved, I'm heartbroken, sick; with Him, I'm well.
   It's as simple as that.

Even though He says, "Don't bring your load of troubles into this Street,"
I will never leave the place in which the Beloved dwells.

While others become slaves to ministers and the king,
Hafiz is slave to the Beloved, and this, to all, he tells.

Learning How to Fly

To the pilgrim, love is the only guide,
And while in the Beloved's path, many tears I've cried.

It's not my fault that I live here in infamy;
I was lost in Love's road, and God was the Guide.

For years now I've been thinking about that ghazal
About the elephant driver on the banks of the Nile who said:

"Either understand the ways of an elephant driver,
Or do not go to India dreaming of an elephant ride.

"Either don't make friends with elephant drivers,
Or begin building a house in which the elephant can reside."

So don't invite me to a Paradise with no wine and no minstrel,
I float better in the winecup than in the salty sea.

Hafiz says: Find the Map of Love and become road-lost,
Or, without the Guide, learn how to fly.

Paradise Face

O Winebringer, if You really love us
Then bring us all the wine you have!

This Winehouse is full of salesmen who sell crystals and healing charms,
But I want only the juice from Your vine.

O friends, you that are alive and still have hearts,
Hear what this drunkard has to say.

You who are crying, give up your wail,
For compared with the world of Love, everything else is pale.

In the path of Love, a poor honest beggar
Is worth more than all the rich man's gold.

O Paradise Face, you ride into town like the Sultan's wife
And the townsfolk follow you around like sheep.

Everyone wants a look at that beautiful face
Shining there behind that veil.

O Master, how many more tears will Hafiz have to cry?
Won't you call for him now that his heart has been broken in two?

I've Said It Before and I'll Say It Again

I've said it before and I'll say it again:
It's not my fault that with a broken heart, I've gone this way.

In front of a mirror they have put me like a parrot,
And behind the mirror the Teacher tells me what to say.

Whether I am perceived as a thorn or a rose, it's
The Gardener who has fed and nourished me day to day.

O friends, don't blame me for this broken heart;
Inside me there is a great jewel and it's to the Jeweler's shop I go.

Even though, to the pious, drinking wine is a sin,
Don't judge me; I use it as a bleach to wash the color of hypocrisy away.

All that laughing and weeping of lovers must be coming from some other place;
Here, all night I sing with my winecup and then moan for You all day.

If someone were to ask Hafiz, "Why do you spend all your time sitting in
The Winehouse door?," to this man I would say, "From there, standing,
   I can see both the Path and the Way."

In the School of Truth

O fool, do something, so you won't just stand there looking dumb.
If you are not traveling and on the road, how can you call yourself a guide?

In the School of Truth, one sits at the feet of the Master of Love.
So listen, son, so that one day you may be an old father, too!

All this eating and sleeping has made you ignorant and fat;
By denying yourself food and sleep, you may still have a chance.

Know this: If God should shine His lovelight on your heart,
I promise you'll shine brighter than a dozen suns.

And I say: wash the tarnished copper of your life from your hands;
To be Love's alchemist, you should be working with gold.

Don't sit there thinking; go out and immerse yourself in God's sea.
Having only one hair wet with water will not put knowledge in that head.

For those who see only God, their vision
Is pure, and not a doubt remains.

Even if our world is turned upside down and blown over by the wind,
If you are doubtless, you won't lose a thing.

O Hafiz, if it is union with the Beloved that you seek,
Be the dust at the Wise One's door, and speak!

I Have Become Famous

I promised the Beloved that as long as my heart beats,
I'd love His lovers as much as I love my own life here in His street.

Because of His candle there is a little light in this closet where I live.
In the moon I can see the reflection of His heart and eyes.

What do I care what the gossips in town think of the way I live?
I have been given this small shelter by You, and it is home.

Not even a hundred beautiful women could lure me from this place,
Could ambush my heart with an army of idols reeking of perfume.

O all you peeping toms, for Christ's sake get some sleep and give your eyes
A rest! And let me have at least one night in silent prayer.

As I walk through the beauty of this world praising Your name,
Not to white rose, red narcissus, or lovely tulip am I drawn—
    but only to Your face.

Hey there, politician, don't tell me I am banned from the Winehouse;
Who died and left you sitting on the throne of God?
I made God a promise, and I'm never going to give up this cup.

It's only fitting that I should praise the Winebringer;
He is my best friend, and His wine is the only wine there is.

No one has a Lover as good as mine!
Why should I be fearful of sin or Satan when to such a Master I can pray?

So, don't worry about Hafiz; from years of abstinence
I have become famous for my drinking and my love.

No Rosary or Holy Coat

O pilgrim, there is something that I want to say:
Since your glass of wine is full, share it with others, that
   they, too, may taste the love of God.

Let those old and with experience do the talking.
To you, young one, I say take my advice and keep silent
   so that you will become old and wise before your time.

The hand of Love doesn't shackle, with chains, he who is sober and full
Of his own wit. If you want to run your fingers through the Beloved's hair,
   then drink!

No rosary or holy coat can give you the high of being drunk;
So go to the Wineseller, He will give you all the help you need.

Don't worry about property and money in this life. Even if you have enough
Friends to sell a hundred houses or family to live a hundred lives, it would
   not pay for His advice.

But be careful, for Satan will tempt you at every turn:
He is everywhere, so be silent and listen for the advice of angels
   and your heart.

Because of all this talk of money, the world has been ruined and there is
Little joy. To remedy this, let's bring out the harp. Beat loudly on the drum!

Winebringer, may Your cup never be empty of wine!
And give me the dregs if that is all you have left.

Even in his shaggy clothes, Hafiz wants to give You a kiss;
He may be drunk, but he will never soil Your flowing gown of gold.

The Monks in the Monastery

Winebringer, come quick! For the Beloved has taken off His veil
And the monks in the monastery have taken all the lamps.

How am I going to see His face with only this small candle?
By the time I get there He will be an old man!

A single glance from the Beloved and all reverence was run off the road.
Enemies of beauty and virtue saw this and moved over into the fast lane.

Because of the birds of grief that had broken our hearts,
God sent us Christ to take up our travail.

O Beloved, now that you are here, under the sun and moon,
Work has taken a new meaning.

The radios of the seven heavens are playing this story over the air waves,
While those with small ears listen to stations only playing silly songs.

Hafiz, where did you learn the magic of writing words?
The Beloved seems to have turned your weary wail into gold!

Plant the Tree of Friendship

Plant the tree of friendship that it may bring fruit to the heart's desire,
And plant it where the shrub of unfriendliness used to be.

When you are a guest here in the Winehouse, it is a rule
That you must respect all drunks, even those drinking from the dregs.

These evenings of wine and song are like gifts
That come unexpected and help keep us awake at night.

O my heart, make a wish for the coming of spring,
That in every field there will be a thousand birds and a hundred roses
    will grow.

O Beloved, my heart has fallen in love with Your hair;
Let them marry so all my restlessness will cease.

O heart, after drinking a hundred gallons, you've fallen under the weight
Of all that wine. Go, and drink one more cup of wine, so tiredness will turn
    to collapse.

Hafiz, here in this garden, ask at least one favor of God:
That you may sit under the cypress and beside the stream of His embrace.

The Only Dervish in the World
Who Can't Dance

I am perhaps the only dervish in the world who can't dance,
Because my heart is like a frightened deer.

In Winehouse Street I walk around weeping, with hanging head,
Ashamed of how little I've accomplished and how little I have done.

The Golden Age of Egypt didn't last forever and neither did Alexander's reign.
O dervish, don't add your troubles to an already troubled world.

Friend, face it, you're a slave, so don't go complaining about
The lack of love in your life: move on!

Hafiz, it's not every beggar who has touched the hem of the Beloved's shirt;
All the gold in the Sultan's bank wouldn't fit into His hand.

Finish This Poem

O lover, what use is there to beg and plead like a madman
When the Creator knows you better than you know yourself?

O King of Beauty, I feel like I'm on fire;
My wine-drenched lips are yearning for the cool breath of God.

O you actors, get out of my sight; I've nothing to say to you!
Who needs enemies when one is surrounded by friends?

Hafiz, finish this poem and don't worry if it's good or bad:
To argue with these pretenders about quality is a waste of time.

These Ghazals

O Beloved, since You took Your shadow from the meadow, the birds
Have taken up their nests and moved away.

The pen of fate won't help you draw beautiful pictures of your desires;
Only God can bring a confession from one who is in love with himself.

Minstrel, change chords and play us that song about the Path:
The one that God walked before He went away.

These ghazals are the songs of Hafiz. He who has never heard
His melodies has never felt heart's fire and then cried.

Like the Morning Breeze

Like the morning breeze, if you bring to the morning good deeds,
The rose of our desire will open and bloom.

Go forward, and make advances down this road of love;
In forward motion, the pain is great.

To beg at the door of the Winehouse is a wonderful alchemy.
If you practice this, soon you will be converting dust into gold.

O heart, if only once you experience the light of purity,
Like a laughing candle, you can abandon the life you live in your head.

But if you are still yearning for cheap wine and a beautiful face,
Don't go out looking for an enlightened job.

Hafiz, if you are listening to this good advice,
The road of Love and its enrichment are right around the curve.

Even the Wealthy Read My Verse

Illiterate and banished from class, the Teacher,
With a single glance, became principal of a hundred schools.

At the same moment, the college of Love and Joy became prosperous,
And its Chancellor became the arch of my Beloved's brow.

For His lovers, the Teacher poured out so much wine
That the scientists became senseless and the philosophers dumb.

Hafiz, for God's sake, clean that wine off your face;
You're so drunk now that even your heart is talking to itself!

Since the Beloved put us drunkards in charge of the Winehouse,
We've hired the oldest beggar in town to be in charge of pouring wine.

Now our Winehouse is the most popular place in town.
Even water and fresh flowers sell here for a thousand bucks.

Yes, even my poems are as precious, now, as gold;
And like magic, even the wealthy read my verse.

Friends, listen to my advice: You'd do best to stay away from the Winehouse.
Look at Hafiz, have you ever seen anyone this strange?

The Rose

Today, the wine in the Winehouse is clear and all the songbirds in the world
Are drunk. This is proof of love's seasons, when love's mystery arrives.

From the corners of the earth, I can smell the scent of happiness;
The breeze has brought it and it smells just like a rose.

O newlywed, stop your complaining. Life's hardships
Are only this bridal dress of beauty and a skillful bride.

O nationalists, don't go making war against small sovereign states;
This outrage of injustice is wrong and there is a heavy price to pay.

All the garden's flowers, in the evening light, look like jewels—
Except the rose, which was sculpted in the image of God.

On the trees that are attached to the world, only the fruit of burden grows.
Happy is the cypress that is free of burden and free of fruit.

O Minstrel, come and sing us some of the sweet songs of Hafiz;
They are full of happiness and timeless in their joy.

Good News!

Good news! These hard times won't last forever;
Good times and bad times are both the same: neither lasts.

To those who gossip, I'm a heathen and as worthless as dust;
But in the Beloved's eyes, they are worthless, too.

Since the doorkeep to this Winehouse is a moral man,
The rich ones with their harems will be chased out with his sword.

O candle! attracting the moth is not a cause for grief.
Celebrate this union, for dawn and the end to self-reflection are near.

Today I got good news from the world beyond the veil: Gabriel told me
That with all the sorrow in the world today, no one will stay.

No matter what the future brings, why be happy or sad,
For even on the pages of the Book of Life the writing will someday fade.

The song at last night's party went like this:
"Bring me the cup of wine, for all this liquid is soon gone."

O strongman, crush this dervish heart with your hands;
Even a warehouse of gold or a storehouse of silver is quickly spent.

On the dome of this Winehouse it has been written in gold:
"We only accept credit cards made from plastic of pure hearts."

This morning, there was more good news: permission to unite with Him.
The message said: "Caught in grief's cage, surrender is your reward."

Hafiz, don't ever stop longing for the wine of the Beloved;
His goodness will wash all this tyranny and violence away!

Good Wine Is Good Company

Since You have promised me union,
What is there left here for me to do?

No wonder Your lovers sit on Your threshold and cry;
Around sugar there are always plenty of ants.

What use is a sword to me now that You have already taken my life?
As Your lover, all I've ever asked for is a glance.

If I could only breathe one breath with the Beloved,
In terms of social security, that would be enough.

Because I am poor and disreputable,
Will my desire alone pay tuition to Your school?

How can a man who is drowning find his way to shore?
The torrent of love's labor is both before him and behind.

I have been Your lover and been with You a thousand times;
Yet each time You see me, Your question is always "Who is he?"

Good wine is good company, and so is the Beloved:
Hafiz has lost his heart to this union and will always be this way.

Hoping Beyond Hope

When the Beloved holds up His glass of wine,
The stock market crashes and a time of darkness comes.

I have fallen into the ocean and become a fish;
O Beloved, throw out Your hook and reel me back onto land.

Everyone who has never seen You has shouted out:
"Call the cops!" and "Take this drunk away!"

Full of grief, I lie here at the feet of the Beloved,
Hoping beyond hope that He will take me by the hand.

Happy is the heart of he who, like Hafiz,
Drinks wine and brings the eye of the Beloved his way.

The Great Forgetter

The moment I touch the tip of Your hair, You run away;
And then if I try to find solace, You criticize me for being sad.

And if I try to sleep after drinking too much wine,
You show up in my dreams, keeping me awake.

And if, during the day, I try to explain my behavior,
You become drowsy and begin to snore.

O heart, the path of love is not paved or cushioned with soft grass,
And he who runs along this rocky road will fall.

When the wind of pride kicks up, all bubbles are burst,
And the one who is thirsty will be told there's no more wine.

Hey, old man, it won't do you any good to boast of beauty and eloquence.
In this world of youth, everyone will laugh.

Even if someone offers you an empire, don't sell your beggar's rags
At the Winehouse door. Do you know anyone who has moved from
   the ghetto to the rich side of town?

They call me "The Great Forgetter," and I'm afraid that now
I'm stuck with this name.

Hafiz says: Come out from behind that veil!
The only thing standing between yourself and the Beloved, is you.

Begging at the Winehouse Door

O God, the beautiful rose that you once gave me,
I am giving back.

In the Winehouse where they drink wine to the memory of Your sweet lips,
Dangerous is the one who is still there drinking and thinking of himself.

It's wrong to solicit and beg at the Winehouse door;
Throw the earnings of these thirsty dogs into the sea!

He who is afraid of suffering can never be a lover:
For these, submission or kissing is the only Way.

These couplets Hafiz writes of grace and knowledge are a mystery.
And they come from the Divine!

It Is Time to Wake Up!

Hey you, parrot! speaking in riddles,
Sugar wouldn't melt in your mouth!

Clear your head so your heart will be happy,
And then mimic the words of the Beloved!

To everyone who walks by, you have given mixed messages;
For God's sake, tell us something we don't know.

O Winebringer, throw some of Your best wine in our face,
For it is time to wake up!

What chord was it last night that the Minstrel played
That caused the drunk and the pious both to dance?

What drug did You put in their cups
That caused them to lose both their hats and their heads?

Not even to Alexander the Great would Your lovers give the Wine of Life;
He hadn't the power or the gold for that price.

Today, reason is the currency of the world,
But compared with Love, even alchemy has lost its flash.

Come, and listen to our stories of pain;
Even with few words, the truth is still there.

O Lord, don't tell our secrets to those who don't drink;
One cannot give a picture on the wall Your enlightened touch.

To a millionaire, money is the standard of the world;
Hafiz says: O beggars, I have exchanged all my money for these poems!

Come Back!

O Beloved, please come back. My heart is broken,
And my body is a wreck and almost dead.

Come back: for I've been blinded from the lack of Your light,
And only light from Your window will open my eyes again.

Like the armies of Egypt, grief has conquered my bleeding heart;
Only Your face, like love soldiers, will free me of this pain.

When I hold up the mirror of my heart,
All I see is Your face.

I sit here counting stars, wishing You would come.
In a night pregnant with possibilities, let's see what this night brings!

O pilgrim, don't worry. This desert is your friend.
God is not hiding there in the sand dunes or in some mirage.

Hafiz, come! The Beloved has tracked you down from the scent of your hair.
He is a lover of ghazals and loves it when you talk this way!

The Letter

Even though I can't read or write, I know no letter came from You today.
Where is that old scribe who has been writing all my notes?
Has he not been putting my letters in the mail?

O Teacher, I know You taught us that we couldn't get to You
Without much effort and without Your help, but all this silence
    is leading me astray.

Maybe if I drink some more from this jug of wine,
Time will pass and a letter from You will come.

Eating candy with this sweet wine will not take this pain away.
Think about tomorrow—it's better to mix something sour
    with what is sweet.

O fundamentalist, get out of this Winehouse while you can;
If you stay any longer, you too may end up drunk and misbehaved.

You've preached to us about the dangers of drink, both night and day;
Now tell us something good. About the Winemaker and the beauty of
    His wine, what have you to say?

O winelovers, in the Winehouse , God is your only friend.
He doesn't come here with pockets filled with trinkets to buy your love.

Remember those wise words the Winebringer last night told the drunk:
"Don't accept wine or the heart of some young punk who can't pray."

Hafiz is consumed by the sun that shines on the Beloved's face.
O postman, don't you have a letter for one who is dying of thirst today?

Bound to Karma

O Teacher, share some of Your wine with Your disciples.
What harm is there in wasting wine this way?

We know that by breaking in love's door, we are bound to karma,
And death will retrieve us: ashes to ashes and clay to clay.

So, drink up! Drink everything you have.
And don't worry, death's sword is dull today.

No matter if you are living in hell or are living in paradise,
In every religion, selfishness is against the Way.

The Architect of the Sky has made this house with six sides,
So that in a world of distraction, in this house you'd want to stay.

Remember: wine charms reason's wits and takes its rust away.
This vineyard will be here from now to Judgment Day!

Hafiz, you chose the path to the Winehouse, happily,
So from this path of prayer and love, don't stray.

Practice What You Preach

Beware these preachers who use altar and pulpit as a stage for a one-act play,
For in their chambers and with friends, they have nothing at all to say.

I say: "You silver-tongued devils,
Go practice what you preach!"

They must not believe in karma or the Judgment Day,
Making all this noise in the name of God.

They brag, today, of their new beach house and their sporty car;
O Lord, teach them a lesson, and tomorrow kick them in the head!

I am a slave to the Beloved. In the Winehouse,
All His lovers are simple folk and are made from Adam's clay.

O monk in the monastery, jump up! The Winebringer
Is making strong wine and He is giving it away!

O greedy ones, go home and clean up your house;
Would you want God to live with all those idols and in all that mess?
And make room for us, so when drunk, we'll have a place to stay.

O Sufi, it's no use, these selfish preachers will never learn to whirl;
They give equal value to the shell as to the pearl.

Hafiz, come sing us some of that lovely verse.
God woke up this morning and decreed that forever this will be your day!

This Cup of Wine Is Like Christ

In the eyes of the pious and the peeping toms, I will never
Be anything other than a drunk.

They watch me night and day, and say:
"No one loves a wino, not even another drunk."

When the hypocrite broke my wineglass, he also broke my heart:
"A tooth for a tooth," was all he said.

This cup of wine is like Christ; by its very nature
It can raise the dead.

O Minstrel, play something beautiful, so that I will
Want to dance like Jupiter and all the stars!

O Master, where do You get all these pearls?
I've given away my life to this diving, and have yet to find a single one!

So pilgrim, put down that book you are reading about money and the rich,
And memorize the lines that are chapters on the Beloved's face.

Hafiz, look for wealth in the Sea of Love, not in the Book of Desire:
Only by swimming naked and diving will you become purified in pearls!

Our Weeping Has Created Oceans

O Master, since You went away, Your lovers are drinking poison
And are dying off like flies—

It's not as if we've been pumping iron, propositioning prostitutes,
And working to get rich!

Why have You abandoned us this way?
Have our weeping and our prayers been too much for Your ears?

Are there not tears in Your eyes, too?

Since our weeping has created oceans,
Why don't You take Your vacation at the beach?

O pilgrims, don't listen to a word the bankers or the lenders say;
God is not vindictive and full of hatred and greed.

All that these lovers of money know is the rattle of coins;
In the vault of their banks, God is nowhere in sight.

Hafiz says: Come here, all of you who are like me, and let's celebrate our
Good fortune. It is in our drunkenness that all our gold resides.

The Chessboard of Lovers

O ignorant one, just because you don't understand our drinking
Is no reason to hate us or spread rumors and lies.

Along the Path, whatever befalls the traveler is for his own good.
It is impossible to lose your way on a straight stretch of road.

To explain this game of life, I will move a pawn:
On the chessboard of drunken lovers, there is no checkmate,
   and no one wins.

What is this room we're in, full of clouds and sky?
To this question there are no answers and no sage who knows the way.

Master, why have You given us the power of free will?
For all its potential, all it does is make us cry.

I guess you could say that the God of Secretaries is illiterate and can't count.
What kind of deal is this? The Beloved hasn't even signed this Deed!

So, if you have something to say, speak up!
Don't be shy. In this courtroom there is no jury and no judge.

And don't worry about how much you weigh and what it is you wear:
On this runway a miniskirt looks good on both fat and skinny legs.

Only those who are pure of heart live on Wineseller's Street,
And fewer still who find their way to the Winehouse door.

Call me the slave of the one who fills our cups with wine.
This wine is for the simple, not those burdened with high religious status
   and degrees.

What does it matter that Hafiz does not sit on some lofty throne?
He sits all day in the Winehouse and drinks the dregs—
   and for this they have made him king!

Look at This

Look at this! The Beloved is drunk, His hair is messed up,
His clothes are torn, and it looks like He's not had a bath in days!

Late last night, at midnight, the Beloved came this way to my bed—
Holding a jug of wine.

He whispered in my ear: "O poor lover,
Are you awake or are you asleep?"

I said; "Whatever You have put into my cup I have drunk without question.
I have been faithful and have never denied my love of wine."

Even though I stay up late at night, and wait,
This drinking has been my fate.

So, go away, preacher, and leave me alone.
Stop giving me hell for drinking only dregs—it's all I can afford.

Everything the Beloved has poured into our cups, we've tried;
Whether it was the wino's brand or the Elixir of Life.

Like the laughter from a cup of wine and the braid of the Beloved's hair,
Hafiz has had a life that is joyous and then has come untied.

Between Two Rivers

Between two rivers, Shiraz is a city built on a holy site.
I pray that it will always be this way.

From somewhere downtown, the scent of ambergris
Always blows refreshing and cool.

Come to Shiraz, all, come!

Why would anyone want sweets from Egypt
When in Shiraz we have lovers of God?

O wind, what news do you bring of
The moon-eyed girl who drinks wine?

Oh please don't wake me from this dream,
For it is sweeter than Shiraz's chocolate on my tongue.

If the pious or even the lovers of wine should kill me,
Then give my blood to beggars like mother's milk to quench their thirst.

O Hafiz, when separation from the Beloved makes you sad,
Remember Shiraz and the time there, together, that you had.

Bad News

Extra, extra, read all about it: the barmaid has taken off her veil!
She has given up heavy drink, and is drinking only wine!

What should we make of this?
Now that she has come clean, why is she going away?

We need her here to fill our cups;
So, Winebringer, demand that she stay!

O Minstrel, sing us that happy song again
To remind us of this drunkenness and the remedy of wine.

Not the seven oceans or a hundred fires
Can remove the bloodstains of wine from the Sufi's coat.

From the clay of my heart and the breeze of the Beloved
A beautiful rose has bloomed and the nightingale celebrates in song.

Hafiz, never give up being humble. Those who have fame and wealth are envious.
They go to church each Sunday. And in going have only themselves
    to blame.

River of Wine

O Beloved, upon this river of wine, launch our boat-shaped cup,
And into this river throw those weeping with envy, too.

Winebringer, throw a cask of wine into my boat,
For without that—for forty days and nights on the open sea—
   I will die of thirst.

I am lost in this city and can no longer find the Winehouse door.
Please help me to find that street again where Love resides.

Bring me a cup of wine that is dark red and smells like musk.
Don't bring me that expensive brand that tastes like money
   and smells like lust.

Even though I am drunk and worthless, be kind to me,
And on this dark heart shine the light of Your smile.

If it's sun at midnight that you desire, throw the veil from
The face of the rose, and you will have all the light you need.

If I die, don't let them bury me in a dusty grave;
Take my corpse to the Winehouse and throw me into a cask of wine!

Hafiz, if you have had enough of this world and all its violence,
Then take up the cup; and from the inside let this liquid love make peace.

No Guarantees

These days the only friend that is faultless
Is a bottle of red wine and a book of poems.

Wherever you are going, go alone; for the road to enlightenment is
Very narrow and full of curves. And take your wineglass with you,
    for there are no guarantees.

I am not the only writer that is worried about having a job.
Knowledge without experience is the "wise man's" fate.

In this noisy street, the voice of reason says:
The world and all its possessions is no security.

Let me tell you an old story: the face of an old camel, destined by
Fate to be black, cannot become white from washing and cleaning.

Everything you see around you will one day disappear,
Except Love, which lasts forever.

I had great hopes that, with my heart, I would unite with You.
But along the Road of Life, death lurks like highway robbery.

I say hold on to the Moon-Faced One's hair, and don't tell a soul!
For the effect of Saturn and the stars, is agony and good luck.

No one will ever see Hafiz sober, never.
He is drunk on the wine of endless Eternity, and keeps asking for more!

The Moon-Eyed Girl

That moon-eyed girl has stolen my heart again!
And has given me nothing but mischief, broken promises, and dark colors
    in return.

And all this after I'd spent a small fortune on her
For expensive silks and cloth, just to be close to her moonlike face.

I guess I should be thankful for the company of an angel
Rather than being stuck in the Winehouse with all those sweating men!

O gypsy girl, have pity on this beggar and wino at your door;
I have given up everything I have. For you!

Say something! Anything hot and sexy will do;
But please, throw no more water on these flames!

Come here! Last night I dreamed I was content
And this surely must have something to do with you!

You and I were destined to be as one,
For it is written in the Book of Dreams.

When I die, tie a cup on my coffin, so that
When I rise from the dead I can quench my thirst with wine.

Hafiz, get up, and run to the Beloved before this goes too far.
Don't be like that silly rabbit who built his lover's likeness out of tar!

On a Road Outside of Town

On a road outside of town at dawn,
A traveler said to his companion:

"O Sufi, the only pure wine is that which
Has been in the jug for forty days."

Unless the seal-ring is on the finger of Solomon's hand,
What special power does that seal-stone convey?

God frowns on those who wear long, loose coats,
Where a slave might have a hundred idols hidden away.

Even though there is darkness within, from Beyond
A lamp can light up the cell of a monk.

Even though generosity is only a word whose origin cannot be traced,
Go ahead and give what you have to those who are hungry and in need.

O Lord of the harvest, if you show a little more attention to the corn-picker,
I'll make sure you get your pay.

Nowhere, today, do I see cheerfulness and ease,
Or medicine for the heart of those without faith.

No hope or dreams,
Or words of love written in blood on any page.

Don't listen to what the wise man says, he doesn't have a clue.
Nor does Hafiz, alone in his cabin and reading all day.

Show me the door of the Winehouse!
So that I can ask the Sage about my fate.

Hafiz says: It is the nature of the beautiful ones to be cruel, so how do
You think they would feel being blessed by a sad, humble man like me?

Talking to the Moon

If ever I get the chance to sit down with The-One-Who-Owns-My-Heart,
From fortune's cup I'll drink my wine and from the Garden of Union
   gather flowers.

That hot Sufi-burning wine is not so strong;
Winebringer, give us a little kiss and take my life in trade.

Loving You this way is driving me mad, for already I
Talk to the moon and see angels in my sleep.

Your lips have been sugar to drunkards and Your eyes like sight to the blind.
Without Your gifts, I have nothing, neither candy nor the wine.

O Winebringer, when I get up from this Winehouse chair, I'm going to the
Palace of the dark-haired girl to give away my life—but only if you promise
   to be the candle beside my bed.

Every grain of dust the wind has brought is a gift of Your grace.
I am an old servant, so don't forget me when I'm out of sight.

Not everyone who writes verses is a poet and is welcomed with applause;
But in this world of illustrious birds, I am a poor falcon and have learned
   to fly fast!

If you don't believe this, then go and ask the greatest painter in China,
For he will tell you he covets the images that come from my pen.

O Winebringer, where are You? Get out of bed!
From last night's drinking, all I hear in my head today is the twang of that
   awful harp!

It's not everyone who is faithful and speaks the truth;
I am the slave of the Chief of the Age, Jalaluddin, the Truth Speaker.

From my pen, listen to the mysteries of love and wine,
For each night you'll find Hafiz drinking with the Pleiades and the moon.

In a State of Drunkenness

O Friend, I hope this road we are traveling goes by the Winehouse,
For we're all thirsty and needing a drink that lies behind that door.

On the first day of our journey we fell into drunkenness and telling lies,
And after we had promised our teachers and families we wouldn't
    come this way.

In this world full of wind, why is it that we go astray?
Better to drink wine and let the chips fall where they may.

In this state of drunkenness, I wonder if we can even hold on to Your belt
Sitting here in the heart's blood like a little red boat.

Preacher, why do you want to always give advice to those who are grieving
And insane? For those of us sitting here in the dust at the Beloved's feet
    are not looking for Eden or some magic lake.

While the Sufis lose themselves in the rapture of the dervish dance,
We are possessed by love's music and lift our hands and sway.

Here in this dust, Your helpless lovers are as valuable as rubies,
On which You have sprinkled wine, today.

O Beloved, please allow us one look at Your face,
For life is short and soon You will be gone.

Hafiz, when the way to the tower of the Beloved's palace is blocked,
Then in the dust of this door's threshold let us put our head and stay.

Forever Young

This morning, while trying to repent, I said: "Hear me, God, and tell me what
To do." But in the middle of this grieving, spring arrived.
   What else can I say?

I'm telling you the truth, this should not be hard for you to understand;
While I sit in renunciation, my friends are all out drinking wine.

O Winebringer, bring me some wine, for I am surely mad
And need Your cure if I am to give up all feasting and happiness for You.

O Beloved, here, let me put this offering upon Your throne of roses
While at the heads of my enemies I am hurling stones.

A necklace of lilies and a bracelet of hyacinths, all for You.
Now I can finally see Your face!

Although I am only a beggar in Wineseller's Street, when I'm drunk
I can control the stars and paint the whole sky blue!

And know that abstinence and deprivation are not my way,
Let the so-called "righteous" make fun of happy drunkards as their play.

Like the laughing lip of the rosebud, I raise my glass to You and drink,
Then tear my coat of rags in two.

Should I be the lucky one to be kissed by the Beloved's red lips,
I swear I'll be born again and become, forever, young!

It is not for us to be judge and jury,
Making profits from the condemnation of the lovers of wine.

Hafiz says: All you charlatans, enough of all this plotting against God!
With only a harp and a single glass of wine, I will expose you and dash
   your dreams today.

Singing Out of Key

O Beloved, come over here so we can throw some roses into Your cup of wine,
And tell us of divine knowledge and the life of the heart before we
    tear off the roof of the sky and go out on the wrong path.

Should a hostile army invade our town and cause the blood of lovers to flow,
The Winebringer and I will go gladly, with our captive friends, to jail.

We'll pour Your rosewater into the muddy water and the cheap red wine,
And change it to sweet sugar that tastes like the blowing breeze.

Minstrel, since you've got your harp in your hand, sing us a song of love
So we can dance, waving hands, as we make our way down the dance line.

O breeze, take our dust to the house of the Beloved,
So that along with the lucky, we, too, may get a glimpse of His face.

While one person boasts of reason, another speaks of inspired trance;
Come, let's take this discourse to God and let Him be the judge.

If it is of Paradise and Eden that you dream, then come with us
To His Winehouse, so we can throw you into the Master's pool from the
    bottom of this wine barrel where you hide.

O Beloved, light up our gathering with the radiance of Your face
And with my head at Your feet, sing my love song all out of key.

Almost nowhere now do they appreciate the art of poetry and spiritual talk.
Hafiz says: Don't worry, to somewhere else that is rich with freedom we will go.

In Hard Times Like These

In hard times like these, listen to this good advice:
Everything I won, I have taken to the Winehouse, where I live in peace.

Except for a jug of wine, a book, and the words I write, I have no friends,
So that the censors and hypocrite wino-watchers will leave me alone.

With my wineglass in my hand, I am far away from judges and righteous saints.
I only hang out, here in the Winehouse, with the pure of heart.

In my old stained coat, I used to be proud of always being right,
But now, in the Wineseller's house with His rosy wine, I am humbled
    and ashamed.

It is my goal to raise my head high, like the cypress, above the clouds.
From this height I can hear the music on the other side of the
    world's sad songs.

Damn this tyranny that covers my heart like dust! Please, God,
Don't let this mirror be clouded by a lack of sun!

This load of grief I carry strains my chest,
And my heart is not the sherpa it once was who could carry this heavy load.

But don't worry, I'm only a servant of the Master of the Age.
If I had any real sense, I'd go searching for relief on High.

So if you see Hafiz as a wineshop drunk or a beggar at the city gate,
Don't worry; he is in no hurry, even though it's getting late.

From the Large Jug, Drink

From the large jug, drink the wine of Unity,
So that from your heart you can wash away the futility of life's grief.

But like this large jug, still keep the heart expansive.
Why would you want to keep the heart captive, like an unopened bottle
    of wine?

With your mouth full of wine, you are selfless
And will never boast of your own abilities again.

Be like the humble stone at your feet rather than striving to be like a
Sublime cloud: the more you mix the colors of deceit, the more colorless
    your ragged wet coat will get.

Connect the heart to the wine, so that it has body,
Then cut off the neck of hypocrisy and piety of this new man.

Be like Hafiz: Get up and make an effort. Don't lie around like a bum.
He who throws himself at the Beloved's feet is like a workhorse and will
    be rewarded with boundless pastures and eternal rest.

This Coat Spun from the Beloved's Hair

O scholar, the fact that I've traded my expensive coat for wine
Is more important than writing this silly book.

The more I think about it, the more it seems I would have wasted my life
Doing anything but drinking and being drunk on the Winehouse floor.

Since the poor never ask for help or advice,
I keep my heart full of fire and my eyes full of water to survive.

I will spare you from my speech about reason and books,
And let you hear it from the harp and the lute, who tell it best.

So, in your head, think of the Winebringer, and in your hand, carry wine.

I swear I'll not buy my heart from any heart-merchant;
I'd rather live in torment and in this coat spun from the Beloved's hair.

Hafiz, it is time for you to leave the Winehouse;
At your age you should leave drunkenness and longing to the young.

True Love

O you who are so full of pride
And without love, get out of my sight.

Don't hang around here with those of us who love the Beloved
And drink wine; surely you are much too smart for that!

Being love-drunk is not something I've imagined or made up.
Go home and quench your mindless thirst on some of your fancy wine.

Those who are truly in love are easy to spot:
With yellow face strained with grief, they stand out in the crowd.

Ask any lover:
The Garden of Paradise is really an empty lot.

O smart ones, we all know of your fame;
Why don't you go outside and try howling at the moon.

Hafiz, it's not a virus or the flu that has made you feel this way;
You are wine-sick, and the only cure for you   is wine.

Now I'm Homeless

O Master, you and I are united in sorrow forever.
I've spent my whole life loving you and have no regrets.

Doesn't everyone know how happy the dogs are in Your street?
If only I were lucky enough to be one of these!

O Beloved, because of all my crying, I gave myself away.
I am love-sick and beyond hope, so have pity.

O young ones, don't think that your beauty, alone, will bring you faith,
For vanity and existentialism are all the rage.

Thirsty for love, we passed by the Water of Life without taking a drink.
O Winebringer, dowse me with the rosewater from Your cup!

O Beloved, I've given up my religion and my worldly goods in order to be
With You, and now I'm homeless and work all day for wine.

If Hafiz dies in the dust of Your doorway, dreaming of Your hair,
He will have lived a full life and died smiling there.

Great Poems

O Master, You are so gracious. After all these years You still
Remember who I am: the one who wears the dust of Your door like a crown.

Tell me, who taught You to be so generous to Your slaves?
Don't worry, I won't tell those spies who are watching Your every move.

O Holy Bird, please bless this path I'm on,
For I'm new to this traveling, and it's a long way I have to go.

O morning breeze, take my prayers to the Master,
And tell Him that each day I am on my knees at dawn.

I yearn for the day when I will leave this house and head out on the road.
When that day comes, friends will wonder where I've gone.

O give me the secret map to the place where I can drink wine with You,
For in that place only can I be drunk, and in my drunkenness be free.

Only great poems can capture the hearts of those who don't read;
So poets, sing! Let the God-of-Oceans fill your mouths with pearls.

O Hafiz, if you are seeking the pearl of union, do this:
From tears, make yourself an ocean   and then dive!

The Cure for Blindness

I must have gone to the doctor a hundred times,
But he's found nothing, no secret potion, for all my grief.

The seal on the coffin of love didn't get there by itself;
It was put there by God's enemies who plotted against Him with fear.

To all you restless roses who have given your power away to thorns,
I say: a nightingale would never give its voice away to crows!

O Beloved, is there no cure for our blindness?
Give us back our eyes so that we may see Your face.

O Physician, even though we have endured our pain of love in silence,
There is no way to hide this much pain from You.

O Friend, at this banquet You have set before us,
How long must we sit here with an empty plate?

Hafiz says: Please believe me, I'm not a hypochondriac and just making
This up. I'm love-sick, and it's those rich doctors who have saddled me
    with shame.

Nothing

The value of all the gold in the world is worthless: nothing.
Winebringer, bring wine! Because this whole world and its business
   is nothing too.

Both heart and soul of Hafiz desire the Beloved's presence.
To him this is everything! And without that, life and happiness are nothing.

Good luck comes to the heart, painless and without blood.
Food picked in the Garden of Paradise gained by blood and stress
   is not real food.

So, if you are tired and hot, don't go looking for shade beneath the Tree of Life
Or beneath the lotus! There is no cool breeze unless you know the Truth.

Life on this earth is short, and is gone, like a forgotten dream.
Use this time to rest, for even this time does not exist.

O Winebringer, we are merely waiting on the shore of the ocean of death.
Fill our cups while You can. Even the time it takes to drink a sip of wine
   is gone too fast.

And friends, don't worry about what people say, be the happy rose.
The power of this passing world is like the breeze—gone—and is nothing.

And I say to the professors: Be careful, and don't always think you are right.
For the distance from the monk's cell to the Master's abode
   is less than you think.

I have been worn away to nothing from all this grief and suffering.
Yet there's no need for me to confess to any priest, for this, too, is nothing.

"Hafiz" is a name that has the seal of approval.
But the wino is not impressed. To have much and to have nothing
   is the same, and is Nothing.

Sun Rays

O Winebringer, the sun is up. Fill my goblet full of wine.
Hurry, for night will come, and then we'll have to sleep.

Outside, the doomsayers are announcing the end of the world.
Quick! give us some of Your delicious wine!

If it is fame and glory that you are looking for from the sun,
Then go back to sleep; there is only divine knowledge in its rays.

When Judgment Day arrives and the sky becomes a jug of poor clay,
Make your skull into a clay cup, and fill it with this pitcher's wine.

Now is not the time to be making small talk with your friends;
Speak only of the cup and of the wine.

Hafiz, get up! Get out of bed. You've work to do,
And the worship of wine is all the worthwhile work there is!

This House Has Two Doors

Do you know what fame and fortune is? It's looking into the Beloved's eyes.
It's preferring a beggar's life to that of being king.

Anyone can kill himself and be lost from this life,
But try giving up friendships or life with one you love!

With my heart closed like a bud, I'll go into the rose garden that is
Full of thorns—to be stripped of my conceit and cocky ways.

O breeze, tell all your secrets to the rose.
Nightingale, sing again the melody of love's sweet song.

Go ahead and kiss the Beloved on the lips.
To pass up this chance is like putting a lock on an open door.

This house has two doors and a dozen windows;
You may never have this chance again.

O Beloved, don't forget to remember the dervish Hafiz;
And send me a postcard if You are ever coming by this way.

This Is a Party

O heart, if you put off today's joy until tomorrow,
Who will insure all that money you've got sitting in the bank?

During the Festival of Life, don't drop that goblet you've got in your hand,
Because you'll need it until the sun goes down and they've brought back
    all the food.

And remember: this rose beside you is as priceless as an expensive gift;
It comes and goes, now visible, now completely out of sight.

O singer, this is a party, so give us your best songs.
Sing us the one that tells of the love we lost and that which is yet to come.

From nothing, into something, in this life Hafiz has come.
Make friends with him now, for soon he will be, forever, gone away.

For All This Writing

For all this writing, they paid me with a branch of sugar cane,
But all the honey and sugar that flows from my pen is my true reward.

Today an angel came to me and gave me some happy news:
"When the world is filled with tyranny and violence, We'll give you
    the gift of patient calm."

It's so much fun being the slave of the Beloved!
For being dust at His feet, I got the highest medal that they give.

That same day, they promised me a life without end;
And all along I had only been able to write of such things!

The moment I fell into the Beloved's trap,
I was released from the chains of anguish and despair.

Because of this blessing and the magic of the sun and moon,
I have been free of the illness of fate and time.

Hafiz, for now at least: rejoice—then scatter the sugar of thanks.
With sweet wine on your lips, you have drunk fully of this life,
    and how sweet it is!

Alchemy

"O drunken friends of mine, bring the wine of the Dawn and let's drink!"
Surrounded by roses, the nightingale sang this song each night.

This bitter wine that the Sufi calls the mother of all grief and pain
Is a far sweeter wine than even a virgin's kiss.

If your life has hit hard times, go to the Winehouse and enjoy some wine.
This elixir can turn even a beggar's meager fortune into gold.

If it's fame and fortune you desire that seems always just out of reach,
Try and change that if you can, but remember destiny.

If the Musician threw a party for all those who loved this ghazal,
Everyone who was pure of heart would dance as He played this song.

The gentle ones who speak only in sweet Persian are the true life-givers.
Wineseller, tell this to all the old teachers and saints, and tell the press;
   this is something that should be written up as news!

Speaking about the Sky

O You, the writing of Mercury is all in praise of Your great glory!
For, truly, You are the author of that book that bears a royal seal
    and speaks about the sky.

Even if You were a poor cypress, you'd make the Tree of Paradise look bad;
Your palace is the envy of every king I know.

Not only are animals, vegetables, and stones Your servants,
But the world of order and chaos   over which you reign!

Both ill and broken, Hafiz became a herald of Your praise.
You are his doctor and his grace, and because of You he's free!

The Only Friends

Ask the sun if you don't believe what it is I say:
The darkness of night is the refuge and companion of pretenders and crooks.

Let go of this nighttime that treats you like poison;
Once you've let it go, sweetness and light will come, you'll see.

Even if you're feeling good, don't stop begging, for treasure only comes
From the glimmering glance of the eyes of the Beloved, who is passing nearby.

O pilgrim who is full of love, choose life; for in the end
The garden is green and the red rose will sooner or later bloom.

Let patience and victory be your loyal companions,
For in the end they are the only friends you need.

No wonder Hafiz sits in his room without a single care;
Whoever goes to the Winehouse will one day, for sure, go mad.

The Ghost of the Winehouse

From the church to the Winehouse our Master came last night.
O friends, now that He's here, what are we going to do?

How can we, now, bow to Mecca,
With the Beloved here and drinking our wine?

Since we are staying here in the Winehouse too,
This must be destiny, and something more than luck.

If only they knew how blessed we are to be chained to Your hair,
The wise would be rushing out and buying chains.

We have fallen prey to the falcon of Your heart:
O Beloved, shake your beautiful hair so that we may take flight!

Your face, alone, contains all the wonder of the Koran;
All we need is grace and beauty to explain this book.

Can You tell us if Your heart of stone can be touched
At all by our hearts that burn and by their flame?

When the wind blew Your hair out of place, my world turned black.
Now I need only a lock of Your black hair to prove to others I am rich.

Hafiz, be quiet! How can you hit the target with arrows made of sighs
And longing? Be sensible and make something aerodynamic out of wood.

Hafiz says: The Beloved has become the ghost of the Winehouse.
I am going to live on the doorstep my whole life and haunt
   this Winehouse, too!

Playing the Game

Hey, Winebringer, bring us some more wine!
Your love at first seemed easy, but now problems have come our way.

Finally I can feel some wind that smells like Your musky hair,
But all that does for my heart is to clot my blood.

Can vagrants like us be happy in Your house,
When each hour a bell rings signaling the end of our stay?

Just say the word and I'll dye my prayer mat the color of wine;
I know how to play this game.

How can those who have died and left us
Know our fear of tidal waves, whirlpools, or the dark night?

By following this path to God, my work has been judged worthless.
How can I keep my love a secret when it's as plain as day?

Hafiz, when you go to the Beloved's house to visit, say goodbye to the world.
If it is the Divine Presence you desire, then you must be prepared to stay!

Go Ask My Tears

O heart, don't walk away from the problems of life:
To the traveler, walking uphill and downhill are both part of the path.

What is there to gain from the wind that brings us only bad news,
When in this garden not even the trunk of the straight cypress gives
    that tree strength?

In this world of illusion, take nothing other than this cup of wine.
In this playhouse, don't play any game but love.

Even though the Beloved's beauty is beyond love,
I'm not going to turn my back on love's game.

With this burning heart, how can I tell you what it is I see?
Go ask my tears, for they are honest and without sin.

Even though we all are taken in by beauty's gaze,
Neither the movie star nor the Wall Street whiz can give us what we need.

If Hafiz is singing his ghazals to the lovers of God,
Not even the voice of Venus could bring down lightning from the sky!

Punishment

If God were to punish us for our each and every sin,
The world would be taken up by weeping and wailing.

In His eyes, the blade of grass and the mountain are the same;
Sometimes He punishes the mountain and sometimes His wrath falls on
    the blade of grass.

Because of our greed, the Earth is covered in blacktop
And the sun eclipsed by the dark of the moon.

Even with a clean shirt, your selfish deeds are not hidden
From He who sees the dirt on your skin.

O Master, forgive me! I promise I will spend each night weeping,
In order that green grass beneath this blacktop can grow again.

And if You leave me, I'll cry such a flood of tears
That no matter where You go, it will rain.

O Hafiz, when the Creator comes for us with death in His eyes,
Who could stand before Him face-to-face and lie?

Hope

On the path to the Winehouse, the fate of those who run
Is the same as the pilgrims on the road to Mecca.

When I was separated from You, I closed my eyes to the world;
But hope of our union has given me back my life.

From now on, I'll go to no one else's door,
For You are the only one I want to see.

I have given up my fortune and have learned how to pray,
And now I can talk to You both night and day.

O Hafiz, your desire for the Beloved is like the wolf who howls at the moon;
Be quiet, and burn like a candle if doubt or violence ever come your way.

Magic Tricks

O Sufi, come and open this bag of tricks;
This is a trap. Release all this sorcery to the sky—

This is like the juggler who hides an egg in his armpit and then
Makes it disappear, and later finds it hidden in his cap.

Winebringer, more wine! The friend of the Sufis is here
And is giving gifts of great beauty and singing songs of grace.

O heart, come here, so we can go over to the house of God
And be far away from all these magic tricks.

Remember, it does not pay to play any games but the Game of Love;
He who makes his own heart disappear is only leaving the door open
    for trouble to get in.

When the truth is known, the magician and the juggler,
For all their tricks, will hide their heads in shame.

O you peacock who struts around proudly, where are you going?
Your pride is vulnerable to even a poor man's prayer.

Hafiz, don't be so hard on God's lovers and those who don't drink wine
Just because you are above hypocrisy and cheap tricks and haven't far to go.

The Greater the Effort, the Worse the Pain

O Beloved, do you think that my love for You is so fickle
That I've forgotten You and have given it away?

I live for You and my heart is love-drunk:
My love for You entered me at birth from my mother's milk.

Love is both its own pain and its remedy;
This irony is almost more than I can take: the greater my effort,
    the worse the pain.

Here, in Shiraz, every night my love-sick cry is the first
One you will hear.

If you added my tears to the Zinda River,
All the farmlands in Iraq would be washed away by flood.

Last night, I swear, I saw the Beloved's face!
With the wind blowing, the clouds were lifted, and it was lit up by the moon.

I went after Him with a passion, my lips ready for a kiss,
But He put me off, saying: "I've got a headache, and it's bad luck to
    make love on a waning moon."

O Hafiz, watch out! Even though you love Him,
The King is all-powerful, and His love can take your life!

Strong Wine

Winebringer, more wine! Bring me some of that strong wine that no one else
Can drink. I want to become unconscious and free of this world for a while.

I know that there's no safety from the perils of the sky,
With the siren harp of Venus and the bloody sword of Mars.

In this age of meanness and deceit, at the world's table,
There is no place for joy. And the food is prepared with too much salt.

So drink wine and wash your palate, so your greedy thirst will go away.

O Sufi, to sit and watch the dervishes won't do you any harm:
Even Solomon the Great found pleasure in watching ants.

Here is a secret that must be kept just between you and me:
The mystery of Time can only be found in a cup of wine.

That is why Hafiz only drinks wine whose color is emerald from a ruby cup:
The snake of this age spits fire, and only this rosy wine can put it out.

Even though the arrow of the Beloved's bow is aimed at Hafiz,
Hafiz says: "I see the muscles in those arms, and it makes me laugh!"

The Pearl

O Beloved, I can see the beauty and grace in that moonlike face;
Won't You share some of those gifts with me?

In the eyes of the law, a child is not even guilty of murder;
So what happens if the one who steals my heart, and kills me, is a child?

Sufi, look out for yourself. Who knows what the child who
Hasn't been taught good from bad will do next?

Knowing this, I have taken a lover only fourteen years old,
Who prays to the soul of slavery and the full moon.

The smell of mother's milk still comes from his lip,
But his black eyes covered with blood give him away.

O Lord, where did we leave our hearts looking for that new rose?
It has been missing now for a long, long time.

O Beloved, if this young lover of mine tries to steal my heart, will You
Send Your palace guards to replace him and then take him away?

O Pearl, with pleasure I would give to You my life,
If You would come to rest in the shell of Hafiz's eye   and stay.

The Essence of Grace

Now that I have raised the glass of pure wine to my lips,
The nightingale starts to sing!

Go to the librarian and ask for the book of this bird's songs, and
Then go out into the desert. Do you really need college to read this book?

Break all your ties with people who profess to teach, and learn from the
Pure Bird. From Pole to Pole the news of those sitting in quiet solitude
    is spreading.

On the front page of the newspaper, the alcoholic Chancellor of the University
Said: "Wine is illegal. It's even worse than living off charity."

It's not important whether we drink Gallo or Mouton Cadet: drink up!
And be happy, for whatever our Winebringer brings is the essence of grace.

The stories of the greed and fantasies of all the so-called "wise ones"
Remind me of the mat-weavers who tell tourists that each strand is a
    yarn of gold.

Hafiz says: The town's forger of false coins is also president of the city bank.
So keep quiet, and hoard life's subtleties. A good wine is kept for drinking,
    never sold.

Forgiveness

Last night the message was sent out from the Winehouse:
"All sins have been pardoned, so drink all the wine you need!"

While bankers and beauticians were doing their own thing,
This news of divine forgiveness came our way.

We should have known all along that the grace of God
Is greater than silence or all our sins combined.

Take these words into the Winehouse
So that the ruby-red wine there will bubble and spray.

Even though union with the Beloved is something they don't give away,
Try as hard as you can till your heart stops pumping blood.

My head is tangled in the curls of the Beloved's hair,
And my face is covered in Winehouse dust.

Hafiz says: Even though the pious say my drinking is a sin,
I know this isn't so—I was born thirsty, and this wine is a gift from God!

The Poor and Pure of Heart

In this city, in all these stores, I have spent
Everything I have, even my last dime.

I'm so hungry now, I'm chewing on my hands for food
And my emotions have turned from callousness into sighs.

Like the rose whose petals fall after blooming,
In my body and spirit I have set a fire.

Last night a nightingale came to my window and sang.
Its song was so sweet I listened, and it had this to say:

"O pilgrim, be happy. Your Beloved is often angry because of
Poverty and bad luck. There is no need for you to act like this!

"If spiritual enlightenment is taking too long and you are tired of the world,
Then give up everything, even your words.

"Even if waves of misfortune were to come crashing on the roof of the sky,
The poor and pure of heart would stay completely dry."

O Hafiz, what if it were possible to achieve union with God?
Do you think that for even a moment you'd continue to behave this way?

Waterboy of the Drunks

O Beloved, when I drink from Your red glass, I lose consciousness.
When I look into Your drunken eyes, I go deaf.

Even though I am Your slave, and useless,
Sell me to the owner of the Winehouse, so I won't be far from Your lips.

Everywhere I go, I carry a wine cask on my shoulder,
Hoping that someone will give me, in exchange, Your cup.

In this street, I am the waterboy of the drunks.
My destination is the Winehouse, and at that door I cry all day.

Don't tell me to meditate or try to hold my breath to remedy my pain.
Would the bird in the meadow take such ill advice?

In all my searching I can't tell the difference between patience and rest.
Even if I wanted to talk about You, who would have the patience to listen
    and understand?

The moral of this story is: Don't give aged wine to those who are heartless:
This wine is too hot for those who are free of pain.

So lovers of wine, drink up! The Beloved has lifted his red glass
And Paradise cannot be, now, far away.

O Hafiz, stop all this talking and tears.
You are the Sultan of Love, so how can you act this way?

The Rose Garden

This morning I went into the rose garden seeking nectar
As a cure-all for my love-sick brain.

Even on this dark night, the red rose I found
Lit up the garden like a lamp.

The light from the rose was so bright it woke the nightingale,
And it began singing one of its thousand songs.

The nightingale's song was so sweet that the narcissus began to cry,
And the tulip drank the narcissus's tears in passion and in pain.

To show her disapproval, the lily stuck out her tongue like a sword,
And, like a bigamist's wife, the anemone opened up her mouth to tell
the world of her travails.

O gardeners, if you are holding a winejug in your hand, you
Are nothing but a drunk. Be like the Winebringer and wrap your hands
around a glass.

Hafiz, learn from the flowers and the Gardener the difference between
Pleasure and joy. And remember: there would be no messenger if there had
been no message sent today.

Don't Worry, Be Happy

If I'm forced to drink musky wine, so be it;
For the taste of fasting and hypocrisy is certainly not sweet.

Even if everyone in all God's creation forbids me love,
I'll do whatever my Beloved wishes, whatever that may be.

Don't worry, be happy for Hafiz; for it is the nature of God
To pardon sin and for lovers to forgive.

He who sits in the center of the Sufi's circle
Sits in hope that his sitting will gain blessings from the Beloved.

To those of you whom God has given beauty and fortune,
What else do you think you need?

With clean air, beautiful scenery, and good wine,
All that's needed for perfection is a joyous heart.

It's true that the bride-of-the-world is beautiful, but be careful,
Because no one will ever tie this beauty's feet.

The earth will never be without flowers and trees,
For as one dies, another comes to take its place.

O beggar, don't ask me what you should do: look inside.
This mirror will tell you all you need to know.

To the moon-eyed girl, I said: "Come on, give us a little kiss.
Your sweet lips will save me from a broken heart."

She only laughed: "Hafiz, I am not afraid of your kiss,
But turn your lips instead to the face of the Beloved!"

Eclipse

O Winebringer, bring me some wine, and one or two cups won't do.
I'm feeling old, so bring me something that will make me feel young.

Wine is the remedy for pain,
So it must be the remedy for old age, too.

If the sun is the wine and the moon is the cup,
Then pour some of that sun into my mooncup and let's cause an eclipse!

Because all this reason is so hard to shake,
Bring that rope of wine for a noose and we'll string it up!

Please dowse this burning heart with water,
And fill me with fire that's more like water, instead.

The rose of my life has left me. I told her: "Go with joy."
Now bring me some wine as pure as rosewater to fill this void.

So what, if the world stops spinning and the birds no longer sing.
As long as the sound of the gulping of wine fills my ears, I am content.

The reason-mongers say that being a wine addict is either right or wrong.
Winebringer, I don't care what they say. Bring me some more wine!

Friends, don't be sad for the time that wine and the wind have blown away;
The sound of the lute and the lyre will bring it back.

Since we can only see the Beloved's face in sleep,
Bring me that medicine that makes sleep come.

Although I'm already a little tipsy, bring me three or four more
Cups of wine so I'll be good and drunk and can disappear.

Winebringer, even if it is a sin, draw two large jugs of wine
From that cask, and bring it over here!

A Flood of Tears

I lay down in the road where she drives to work,
But she never came.

I prayed for a hundred kinds of kindness,
And she never even looked my way.

O Master, protect me from this young beauty;
All I do all day is sit here and sigh.

Even a flood of tears hasn't washed the hardness from her heart.
No impression on that stone was ever made by rain from the sky.

As a candle wick drowns in its own wax, I want to die at her feet,
But neither she nor the breeze pass by this morning where I lie.

O my soul, who is so hard-hearted and stupid that he
Wouldn't make a shield against the arrows she let fly?

Last night I cried so hard that neither fish nor fowl could sleep,
But that young lovely, sleeping, never even blinked an eye.

O you young thing, behold the bird of my heart with its wings and
Feathers consumed. Get out of my head! You are driving this lover mad.

Poor Hafiz! We all know your sad story of love,
But there is nothing that we can do to help.
If given the choice, all we'd want to do is die.

Ransom

Everyone who is a true lover of God
Will be spared from the world and its wicked ways.

I'll only talk about God when He is in the room;
For anything else, He'll have to tell you Himself.

If you don't want God to break His promises,
Then hold on to that cord!

O Sufi, on this precipice live your life in such a way that if your foot
Should slip, angels will pray for your safety and break your fall.

O breeze, please help untangle my heart from the Beloved's hair
And help it find its way.

My mind, heart, soul, and all my possessions are my ransom for His love.
Who has the right to any of this but He?

Even the Master's Private Guard
Is protected by His prayers.

O Hafiz, you are lost, and the path to the Winehouse is nowhere in sight;
Your friend, the wind, got here first and has blown it all away.

The Drinker of Dregs

In life, pure wine and the Winebringer are obstacles along the way
From whose noose even the wise ones will one day swing.

I am an outlaw, a lover, and a drunk who cannot read.
Thank God I am not living in the city in sin.

If you are coming to the Winehouse, come with respect.
If you are a friend of the king, then you will not get in.

It's not natural for either the dervish or the pilgrim to be cruel;
So Winebringer, bring wine, for your lovers are never led astray.

Even if His slaves and servants leave Him,
God goes on about His work as if nothing had ever changed.

Don't think that the drunks and the beggars in the Winehouse door
Are contemptible, for they are beltless kings and crownless monarchs
    in disguise.

Wake up! and spare us from all your hot air and pride,
For there is not enough barley in a thousand harvests to pay for
    all this wine!

Unlike those who wear blue gowns or black hearts on their sleeves,
I am of only one color and am the drinker of dregs.

The Beloved told Hafiz: "Make up your mind; to reach nirvana is a lofty goal.
To get there, get out that map of love and find your way back to Me!"

From the World of Mysteries

O wind, from the road where the Beloved has walked, bring me
A scent of His sweet perfume.

And take this grief from my heart. Replace it with news
Of where He last spent the night.

Tell me something He has said, or from the world of mysteries
Bring me a letter written with love.

O breeze, for this blind man, bring dust where His
Feet have trod, as liniment for these eyes!

O Hafiz, don't be foolish;
Your Lover is not going to pass this way.

Get out of the road. You're blocking traffic and
Causing confusion with all this talk about perfume!

O breeze, I beg you, bring me something I can worship,
Even if it be only a speck of dust.

This separation has made me thirsty.
Winebringer, more wine! And bring that cup of mirrors too.

O birds of the woods, be thankful that you are free
And so full of joy. For those captured in cages only sing of grief.

There's a limit to my patience, and I can feel
The bitterness filling up my heart.

O candyman, bring me some sugar from the Beloved's lip;
My love-disease is tired of so much salt!

I've had enough. Untie my hands, and make a noose from the Beloved's hair
So I can hang myself and forever be free of pain.

O Hafiz, in hot weather, what use is this ragged coat that is dyed in wine?
Who will you impress? Take it to the marketplace if you want to know,
   and see how much it brings.

They've Locked Me Up

Winebringer, bring me a glass of wine that's on fire!
Being here with all these Perfect Masters has made me insecure.

Today I made the mistake of using the first-person possessive when using
His name, and the stares and jeers from the Winehouse patrons felt like a
   whip of nine-tails on my skin!

If that weren't enough, I called Him, wrongly, by my name.
Now the Wineseller ignores me and won't fill my cup.

They've locked me up, now, in the attic, and
I can hear them downstairs laughing, night and day.

O Winebringer, have mercy! This is torture, living
Here in the shadows without a drink.

Who was it that said: "Give me your heart and soul and I will give you peace"?
What a crock—I gave You my soul and all I got was grief!

The tale of wine and kisses from the Beloved has flowed from Hafiz's pen,
But with hand tired and fingers sore, he wants to know:
   when will this sad story end?

Be a Friend of Wine

In the spring when tulips bloom is the time for drinking wine!
Don't be a hypocrite; make friends, too, with roses and the wind.

I'm not saying you should drink wine all year long;
For nine months go on the wagon, and then for three months
    you can be a drunk.

If while on the road a holy fool should offer you a drink of wine,
It's OK, you can trust him, go ahead and drink!

If it is your dream to be wed to the Great Mystery, then come,
But first be a friend of wine, before you go out doing good.

Like the rosebud, the world and its business is closed up tight,
So be like the spring breeze and open up that bud!

If you think you will be thanked or rewarded for your deeds,
Then you are even dumber than I thought and like the fool looking
    for the phoenix or the alchemist's formula for gold.

Hafiz, beware of strangers bearing gifts;
But tell those who love wine that they can forever be your friend!

Thirst

O wind, can't you see I'm sick from grieving?
Please bring me anything, even a brick from His street.

I'm so thirsty for love I'd drink my own blood
Or drink dust from the Beloved's door.

I'm so blind, I've gone to war with my own heart;
Bring me a bow and arrow to defend myself from this pain.

I've spent my whole life wandering, and now I'm an old man.
I'd even drink wine from the hands of a teenager if it would perk me up!

If I go down, I'm going to take the hypocrites down with me, too.
Make every one of them drink a whole jug of wine—and if they refuse,
    bring them here to me!

Winebringer, don't put off until tomorrow what you can do today.
Bring me proof from the Book of Life that my future and my fate
    are written in blood.

Hafiz says: If it's illusion that you want, go get up on that screen!
You'll find me in Winestreet laughing, drunk on His perfume!

This Is the Night of Love

This is the night of Love, and we're closing all books.
We're closing the door of separation, and are letting in the dawn.

O pilgrim, work hard and your heart will strengthen,
And your feet will never trip you up along the way.

O lover, I promise I'll never turn my face away from you again,
Even if you stone me or with curses drive me away.

O friend, if you've given away your heart and gotten
Nothing in return, then it's your right to bitch and to complain!

O daylight, where have you hidden my heart?
In this darkness the only dreams I have are of the night.

Hafiz says: Listen—this is what I have to say.
Love from the Beloved is like business. Sometimes there is profit
    and sometimes loss, and both the good and the bad have come to stay!

Learning to Fly

I traveled a thousand miles to see a therapist about my pain:
After months of tests and listening, he didn't have a clue.

The only thing he said that was intelligent was
That the turquoise ring on my finger   was blue.

It's a shame that there is so much ignorance in the world
Among those who think they are always right.

Hafiz, now that you've traveled and heard the yelps of the world and all
Its strutting birds, go back to the Falconer and be His bird, and fly!

Searching for Truth

All over town, people call me a ladies' man and a lover.
I don't understand—I don't despise them and am not jealous of their ways.

I'm faithful and happy even with all this talk.
"Don't worry, be happy" is my motto, and I'm not deceived.

When I asked the Winemaster about the path to Truth,
He told me to keep quiet and took my glass of wine away.

To prove His point, He poured my wine into the water
Destroying my reflection, and I lost all sense of who I was.
"Now," He said, "you can search for truth."

O Beloved, I have tied my trust to the tip of Your long, flowing hair;
Why should I do anything else? For without You, I don't exist.

But the beautiful soft cheek of a lover teaches us how to also love the
Friend. To praise her beautiful face is praising His face, too.

Today, instead of going to church, I'm going to the Winehouse
To drink some wine. I don't have time to listen to those jobless preachers
   and their empty words.

Hafiz, kiss only the Beloved's lips and drink only the Beloved's wine,
For He is the only reverend, and His wine is the only sacrament you need!

The Cost of a Kiss

I said: "O Beloved, look at me. I am healthy and prosperous.
     When will I get Your kiss?"
He said: "Would I lie to you? While you were talking,
     I kissed you and at the same time took your purse of gold."

I said: "Your price is high. Even if I owned all of Egypt
     I couldn't pay You for that kiss."
He said: "Don't worry, the bankers of Egypt won't lose money
     on this deal, and I won't give you any more than you can take."

I said: "How will I find, then, the way to Your mouth?"
He said: "I will give you a map that only the sensitive can read."

I said: "And how do I avoid idiots and idols along the way?"
He said: "In the Street of Love there are those who tell stories, and
     there are those who tell the truth."

I said: "But I am happy here in the Winehouse. Why would I want
     to go away?"
He said: "Then stay here if you are happy and truly feel this way."

I said: "What do wine and all the preacher's robes have to do with religion?"
He said: "This is like kindergarten to get into the Master's school."

I said: "And what are You doing for those who are old and infirm?"
He said: "With a sweet kiss I will make them feel young."

I said: "And when will we see this kind Master standing at our door?"
He said: "Not until Jupiter collides with the moon, or until
     you can drink a cask of wine."

I said: "But Hafiz prays every morning for Your happiness and health!"
He said: "Don't pray for me; I pump iron and laugh a lot, and have angels
     that pray for me all day. Think of this—now what do you have to say?"

The Fortune-teller

In the days when kings were honorable, fair, and forgiving,
Professors, priests, and Hafiz all drank from the same cup.

Even the Sufi came out from his cloister when he saw the policeman
Carrying a cask of wine on his shoulder, and had a drink!

One day, I asked the Wineseller if the priest and judge
Snuck around like the hypocrite and drank in secret.

He said; "Hafiz, you are above all that; it's not worth your time.
Just keep on drinking and leave them to their deceitful ways."

Winebringer, more wine! Soon it will be spring and there will be
No more wine. Tell me what I should do about my burning heart.

I'm doing everything I can to cover up my trail;
Love, poverty, youthfulness, and spring fever are my excuse.

Friends, be quiet. The moth of our affection is coming. With your
Tongues stuck out so far into the flame of the candle, how will we
    lure Him here to stay?

Believe me, this discipline is worth your silence.
We have never had One like this around here before!

Stay a little longer; He will get here soon.
Don't be taken in by the hypocrites over in the corner
    with their blue coats made to look like the sky.

A long time ago, I went to the fortune-teller to have my fortune read.
She said: "Go to the Winehouse and drink a cup of wine."

Hafiz has been here ever since. He is through with his love of
Suffering and the words that describe that love, and he's
    going to stay that way!

No Fear

O Beloved, even against a thousand armies,
With You on my side I have no fear.

The promise of union with You has kept me alive,
And fearing separation from You, many deaths I've already died.

If the breeze should take away Your scent,
For each breeze that blows I'll make a rip in my Sufi coat.

Do You think that I've been lying around sleeping all these years? Never!
Or that I've learned to be patient from all this separation and all this pain?
    Lord, no!

To be cut wide open by Your hand is better than another's cure.
Your poison is better than anything the pharmacist prescribes.

They say that death from Your sword gives everlasting life.
If this is true, then I'd be more than happy to die.

O Horseman, here are my hands—tie them with Your reins.
And here is my head—against another's sword use it as Your shield.

Hafiz says: Who really knows You as You really are?
It's like the blind telling the blind what it is they see.

Writing Poems from the Light of Your Face

Since I can't even run my fingers through Your hair,
O Beloved, what am I to do?

Everything I do is because of You.
Is this rising and falling to be my only fate?

After drinking a hundred cups of my heart's blood, I finally caught
Hold of Your robe, and now for nothing, for no amount of gold,
    will I let it go.

O Beloved, tonight I will write my poems from the light of Your face,
Rather than from the moonlit sky.

And I will give my clothes and possessions to the minstrels and singers
In order that I be worthy of Your grace.

What can I say? Your tenderness is so subtle
That to even pray now seems like a waste of time.

The face of the Beloved can only be seen by those who are pure,
So don't waste your time looking unless your mirror is completely clean.

O Beloved, You are loved by all the world.
How can I compete with so many, fighting night and day?

Hafiz says: O pilgrim, give up your religion.
Love is a mystery, and like light upon your face, it plays.

Perfect Songs

O Master, there's no more need for wine or minstrels;
Lift that veil from off Your face. I want to dance tonight
    like popcorn on a hotplate!

In truth, no face has the right to become a mirror of the future
Unless it has been kicked by Your horse.

No matter what happens after this, I have told the truth:
I'm running out of patience. How much longer do I have to wait?

O hunter, be compassionate.
Don't aim your gun at the Beloved, who is my deer!

I am only a dirty wino who can't even raise his head from the
Winehouse door. If this is true, then how am I going to
    kiss the Beloved's face?

I know my ghazals are not always loving and worthy of You.
O Beloved, I promise, from now on, I'll only sing You perfect songs.

But my heart is so wrapped up in chains
That I have little more to say.

Hafiz, don't give up hope or stop writing your great ghazals.
Even though you are not free and in love, you are better off in jail.

One Hundred Drops of Blood

Oh no! The wind has stopped blowing.
How, now, will my ghazals or my words ever get to You?

What else is there for me to do but to sit here and cry?
I wouldn't wish this sadness on even my worst enemy.

You are far away, and day and night I lie grieving.
And why shouldn't I, when my heart says there is no hope?

O Beloved, where are You? Since You left,
My heart has become a fountain, and blood is pouring from my eyes.

From the root of every eyelash trickles a hundred drops of blood,
And from my heart pour gallons more!

Hafiz has become a slave to this grieving. In the winecup
He can see his past, and he thinks about it night and day.

The Proof

If I happen to make it over to Your street,
I would consider myself blessed to share with You my poems.

Like the color and scent of the sweet narcissus that stands out from
Other flowers, the sight of You has kept me from sleep.

Because the jewel of Your love has given polish to my heart,
It's also clean of the rust of trouble and defeat.

My life will only be complete after I have lost it
To misfortune and given my desires away.

What have I done that was so bad that
You won't even accept my gifts or recognize my name?

This is Hafiz, and I am standing at Your door.
Where else is there for me to go?

Where will I go, what will I do, what will I be, what will be my plan?
I'm sick of all this sorrow and deceit.

I am the King of Hearts; ask anyone.
No one has suffered this much pain!

Here . . . here are Hafiz's poems. They are proof of my devotion and my love.
I offer them in silence, and they're all I've got to say.

About Hafiz

HAFIZ WAS BORN IN SHIRAZ around the early fourteenth century as Khwaja Shamsuddin Muhammad. At a young age he showed a genius for poetry and was drawn both to Persia's great poets and to the spiritually advanced saints and masters. His favorite poet was Sa'di, who had died a generation earlier but whose verse was sung and praised throughout Persia. Hafiz dreamed of becoming a great poet like Sa'di or Rumi. He also loved the Koran, and while still a boy he learned it entirely by heart—hence the pen name he later adopted, Hafiz, which means "the Preserver" and implies one who has memorized the Koran.

Because of his father's untimely death and the family's subsequent descent into poverty, Hafiz was forced to leave school in his teens and go to work in a drapery shop and later a bakery to support the family. By the age of twenty-one he had become fluent in Arabic and Turkish and was self-taught in the skills of jurisprudence, mathematics, astronomy, and other sciences, and was writing poems under the pseudonym of Hafiz.

Legend has it that as a young man, Hafiz fell intoxicatingly in love with a beautiful young woman named Shakh-i-Nabat ("Branch of Sugarcane"). He became so obsessed with her beauty that he couldn't eat or sleep and began writing poems about her. Since the girl had been promised in marriage to the prince of Shiraz, in desperation Hafiz sought help at the tomb of a great Sufi master, Baba Kuhi, near Shiraz. Before he died, Baba Kuhi had promised that anyone who could stay awake for forty consecutive nights at his tomb would be granted the gift of poetry, immortality, and his heart's desire.

Wanting, really, only to win Shakh-i-Nabat's love, Hafiz completed the forty-day vigil and is said to have then been visited by the Angel Gabriel, who gave him a cup to drink from, containing the Water of Immortality. Hafiz was so astonished by the beauty of the angel that he forgot the beauty of Shakh-i-Nabat, and when Gabriel asked him to express his heart's desire, he replied: "I want God!" Although Hafiz's desire for Shakh-i-Nabat went unrequited and he married someone else, they would remain close, life-long friends.

After the forty-day vigil, Hafiz was sent by Gabriel to a Sufi master of the Ruzbihaniyya order named Shaykh Mahmud 'Attar, with whom he spent the next several years and from whom Hafiz would eventually receive the mantle of God-realization. His fame quickly spread far and wide, and his poems of longing and love for the Beloved were sung throughout Shiraz and beyond.

Word soon reached the court of Shah Abu Ishak, a great patron of the arts who invited Hafiz to recite his verse at the palace. Hafiz's poems—which were uncensored and outspoken in their criticism of the deceit and hypocrisy of the court artists, clergy, scholars, and judges—aroused much jealousy and suspicion. Even so, his reputation grew, and he was able to earn ample money from court patronage of his poetry as well as by teaching at a theological college.

In 1353, Shiraz was invaded and conquered by a robber-prince named Mubariz. As a strictly orthodox Muslim, he closed the taverns and wine shops and instituted laws that deprived Hafiz of his position as a professor of Koranic studies. Hafiz took up work as a calligrapher and a copier of manuscripts to support his wife and child. During the dictatorial rule of Mubariz, Hafiz began writing protest poems, which would eventually make up a sizable portion of his *Divan*.

By the 1360s, although Mubariz had been deposed, Hafiz had made enemies of many members of the clergy as well as poets who were envious of his success. With increasing danger to himself and his family, Hafiz fled Shiraz in 1368 and lived for about four years in exile some three hundred miles from home—giving rise to poems of homesickness for Shiraz and his friends and students.

Since Hafiz was now famous throughout all of Persia, a controversy over his exile raged, with people from all walks of life taking sides either for or against the master poet. In 1375, Hafiz was invited back to Shiraz in order to quell the fiery debate and was reinstated at his teaching position at the college.

By this time, for over thirty-five years Hafiz had been the faithful student of 'Attar, yet he had still not attained his desire for union with God. When Hafiz would ask 'Attar when he would get his wish, 'Attar would simply say, "Be patient, and one day you will know." Nearing the fortieth anniversary of his first meeting with 'Attar, Hafiz began a self-imposed penance in which one draws a circle on the ground and then sits within it for forty days without food or drink and without leaving the circle for any reason. It was said that if a person could succeed in this difficult practice, God would grant whatever he desired. Hafiz remained within the circle for thirty-nine days, and on the fortieth day, Gabriel was again sent to him and asked him his heart's desire. Hafiz's reply was, "My only desire is to wait on the pleasure of my Master's wish." With that, Hafiz was released from the circle and rushed to 'Attar's house. 'Attar embraced him and gave him a drink of wine, making him immediately God-realized. Hafiz had received his heart's desire after forty years of waiting.

Hafiz lived for eight more years, during which time he wrote over half the poems that would eventually be associated with his name. The poems written after his becoming God-realized are written from a state of Divine Knowledge and are much different in tone and content than those written during his days of longing and protest.

Using his poetry as a vehicle for his teaching, for the remainder of his life Hafiz taught in relative seclusion; disciples and other people traveled from all over Persia to be in his company.

Around 1389, after suffering from a long illness, Hafiz passed away. Thousands attended his funeral and his entombment at the foot of a cypress tree he had planted, surrounded by a garden of roses. The tomb and garden became a place of pilgrimage, and soon his name and fame spread beyond the Persian-speaking world. Today the Western world is discovering Hafiz and embracing him as one of their own. His *Divan*, now, as it was following his death, is often consulted as an oracle by students and spiritual seekers around the world.

This biographical sketch is a synthesis of the available reports on Hafiz's life, based essentially on oral history and legend. My chief reference was Paul Smith's Book of the Winebringer *(Melbourne, 1988), which is primarily about the symbolic imagery used in Persian poetry but also includes a history and a small selection of Smith's versions of poems from the* Divan.

About Thomas Rain Crowe

Tₕₒₘₐₛ Rₐᵢₙ Cᵣₒwₑ is a poet, translator, editor, publisher, recording artist, and author of eleven books of original and translated works. During the 1970s he was editor of *Beatitude* magazine and co-founder and director of the San Francisco International Poetry Festival. In the 1980s he was a founding editor of *Katuah Journal: A Bioregional Journal for the Southern Appalachians* and founded New Native Press. In 1994 he founded Fern Hill Records (a recording label devoted exclusively to the collaboration of poetry and music) and his spoken-word and music band, the Boatrockers. In 1998 his book *The Laugharne Poems* (which was written at the Dylan Thomas Boat House in Laugharne, Wales) was published in Wales; his groundbreaking anthology of contemporary Celtic-language poets, *Writing The Wind: A Celtic Resurgence* and his first volume of translations of the poems of Hafiz, *In Wineseller's Street*, were released. He has also translated the work of the French poets Yvan Goll, Guillevic, Hughes-Alain Dal, and Marc Ichall. Following six years as editor-at-large for the *Asheville Poetry Review*, Crowe has recently released a CD recording with his band The Boatrockers titled, *The Perfect Work: Poems of Hafiz*.

Printed in the United States
by Baker & Taylor Publisher Services